family handyman

109 BEST WEEKEND PROJECTS

THUNDER BAY
P·R·E·S·S
San Diego, California

Thunder Bay Press
An imprint of Printers Row Publishing Group
10350 Barnes Canyon Road, Suite 100, San Diego, CA 92121
www.thunderbaybooks.com

Copyright © 2016 Trusted Media Brands, Inc.

All rights reserved. No part of this publication may be reproduced, distributed, or transmitted in any form or by any means, including photocopying, recording, or other electronic or mechanical methods, without the prior written permission of the publisher, except in the case of brief quotations embodied in critical reviews and certain other noncommercial uses permitted by copyright law.

Printers Row Publishing Group is a division of Readerlink Distribution Services, LLC.
Thunder Bay Press is a registered trademark of Readerlink Distribution Services, LLC.

The Family Handyman is a registered trademark of Trusted Media Brands, Inc.
Home Service Publications, Inc. is a subsidiary of Trusted Media Brands, Inc.
Reader's Digest is a registered trademark of Trusted Media Brands, Inc.

All notations of errors or omissions should be addressed to Thunder Bay Press, Editorial Department, at the above address. All other correspondence (author inquiries, permissions) concerning the content of this book should be addressed to Reader's Digest Trade Publishing, 44 South Broadway, White Plains, NY 10601.

Thunder Bay Press
Publisher: Peter Norton
Associate Publisher: Ana Parker
Publishing/Editorial Team: April Farr, Kelly Larsen, Kathryn C. Dalby
Editorial Team: JoAnn Padgett, Melinda Allman, Dan Mansfield

The Family Handyman
Editorial and Production Team
Vern Johnson, Peggy McDermott, Rick Muscoplat, Marcia Roepke,
Mary Schwender

Photography and Illustrations
Ron Chamberlain, Tom Fenenga, Bruce Kieffer, Mike Krivit, Don Mannes,
Ramon Moreno, Shawn Nielsen, Doug Oudekerk, Frank Rohrbach III,
Eugene Thompson, Bill Zuehlke

Library of Congress Cataloging-in-Publication data is available upon request.

ISBN: 978-1-68412-946-1

A NOTE TO OUR READERS: All do-it-yourself activities involve a degree of risk. Skills, materials, tools and site conditions vary widely. Although the editors have made every effort to ensure accuracy, the reader remains responsible for the selection and use of tools, materials and methods. Always obey local codes and laws, follow manufacturer instructions and observe safety precautions.

Printed in China

23 22 21 20 19   1 2 3 4 5

Table of Contents

Storage & organizing solutions

Special section: **2-hour (or less!) laundry room improvements**

Kitchen & bath upgrades

Landscaping & backyard projects

Special section: **Afternoon ponds, fountains & gardens**

Garage improvements

Quick fixes

Special section: Easy lighting upgrades

Fast furniture

Bonus section: Paint anything guide

CHAPTER

1

Storage & organizing solutions

If your stuff is getting the best of you, take charge right now! Here are 18 super-easy projects that can help you take control of your clutter today. These simple cabinets, shelves, racks and organizers are quick and inexpensive to make. Why spend big for ready-made items when you can quickly and easily make something designed just for your needs?

There's also a Special Section on laundry rooms, with simple ways to add more clothes-hanging space, stabilize a front-load washer and dryer, and store laundry products. Each project takes one morning or less!

- -

SPECIAL SECTION:
2-hour (or less!) laundry room improvements

10 *one-morning (or less!)* storage projects

Smart ways to expand and organize your storage space

Stud-space cabinet

When you can't find a convenient nook for a set of shelves, you can often create one by recessing the shelves into the wall itself. Choose the location before you build the project to make sure it will fit. Start by looking for a space with no obvious obstructions. Locate the studs with a stud finder. Some stud finders can also locate electrical wires and plumbing pipes inside walls. When you've found a promising spot, cut a 6-in.-square inspection hole between the studs. Use a flashlight and a small mirror to inspect the stud cavity for obstructions. You often can modify the size of the cabinet to avoid obstructions.

When you find a good space, mark the perimeter of the opening and use a drywall keyhole saw to cut it out. Measure the opening and subtract 1/4 in. from the height and width to determine the outer dimensions of your cabinet.

For standard 2x4 stud walls with 1/2-in.-thick drywall, build the cabinet frame from 1x4s that measure 3-1/2 in. wide (see illustration). If your walls are different, adjust the depth of the frame accordingly. Then add a 1/4-in. back. Screw 1/4-in. pegboard to the back so you can hang stuff from pegboard hooks.

Add casing that matches the trim in your house. Drill holes into the sides to accept shelf supports. Shelf supports fit in 3mm, 5mm or 1/4-in. holes depending on the style.

Install the cabinet by slipping it into the opening, leveling it and nailing through the trim into the studs on each side. Use 6d finish nails placed every 12 in. along both sides.

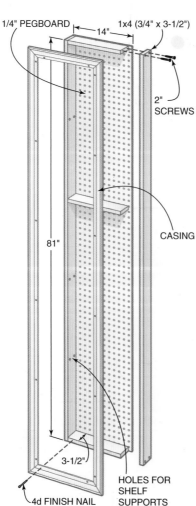

1/4" PEGBOARD
14"
1x4 (3/4" x 3-1/2")
2" SCREWS
CASING
81"
3-1/2"
HOLES FOR SHELF SUPPORTS
4d FINISH NAIL

Bonus storage space! Take a few hours and remove the drywall from between two studs, then construct a shallow cabinet to fit the space.

Heavy-duty utility shelves

Store-bought shelving units are either hard to assemble, flimsy or awfully expensive. Here's a better solution. These shelves are strong and quick to build. Size this sturdy shelf unit to hold standard records storage boxes. If you want deeper storage, build the shelves 24 in. deep and buy 24-in.-deep boxes. If you prefer to use plastic storage bins, measure the size of the containers and modify the shelf and upright spacing to fit.

Refer to the dimensions below to mark the location of the horizontal 2x2 on the back of four 2x4s. Also mark the position of the 2x4 uprights on the 2x2s. Then simply line up the marks and screw the 2x2s to the 2x4s with pairs of 2-1/2-in. wood screws. Be sure to keep the 2x2s and 2x4s at right angles. Rip a 4 x 8-ft. sheet of 1/2-in. MDF, plywood or OSB into 16-in.-wide strips and screw it to the 2x2s to connect the two frames and form the shelving unit.

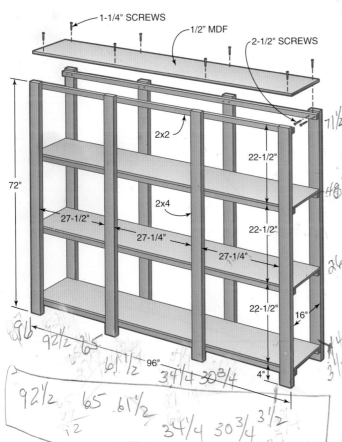

Build sturdy, simple shelves, custom sized to hold boxes or other storage containers.

> **tip** **Labeling plastic bins**
> If you choose plastic bins rather than cardboard storage boxes, label the plastic with a wet-erase marker. When it's time to relabel the bin, just wipe away the marks with a damp rag.

Behind-the-door shelves

The space behind a door is another storage spot that's often overlooked. Build a set of shallow shelves and mount it to the wall. The materials are inexpensive and you'll be finished in just a couple of hours. Measure the distance between the door hinge and the wall and subtract an inch. This is the maximum depth of the shelves. Use 1x4s for the sides, top and shelves. Screw the sides to the top. Then screw three 1x2 hanging strips to the sides: one top and bottom and one centered. Nail metal shelf standards to the sides. Complete the shelves by nailing a 1x2 trim piece to the sides and top. The 1x2 dresses up the shelf unit and keeps the shelves from falling off the shelf clips.

   Locate the studs. Drill clearance holes and screw the shelves to the studs with 2-1/2-in. wood screws. Put a rubber bumper on the frame to protect the door.

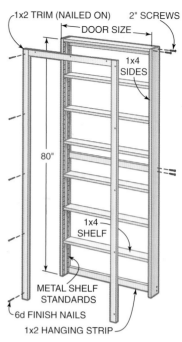

The space behind a door is another storage spot that's often overlooked.

tip **Stud-space shelves**

Open wall framing in a basement or garage makes ideal storage space for narrow items like cleaning supplies or small boxes of nails and screws. Simply cut 2x4s to fit between the studs and toe-screw them in to form shelves.

Build shallow shelves to fit behind the door in your laundry room, utility room or pantry.

Got a half-hour? Screw 3/4-in. plywood to the back of a door to provide a solid mounting base for screw hooks, baskets or other storage accessories.

Back-of-door organizer

The back of a door that opens into a utility room or closet makes a handy hanging space. The trouble is that most doors don't offer a good mounting surface for hardware. The solution is to screw a piece of 3/4-in. plywood to the back of the door. Add construction adhesive for hollow-core doors. Cut the plywood 3 or 4 in. shy of the door edges to avoid conflicts with the doorknob or hinges. Now you can mount as many hooks, magnets and other storage gizmos as you like.

Double the shelf space in your closet in a jiffy by adding a second shelf above the existing one.

Two-story closet shelves

There's a lot of space above the shelf in most closets. Even though it's a little hard to reach, it's a great place to store seldom-used items or off-season clothing. Make use of this wasted space by adding a second shelf above the existing one. Buy enough closet shelving material to match the length of the existing shelf plus enough for two end supports and middle supports over each bracket. Twelve-inch-wide shelving is available in various lengths and finishes at home centers and lumberyards. Cut the supports 16 in. long, or place the second shelf at whatever height you like. Screw the end supports to the walls at each end. Use drywall anchors if you can't hit a stud. Then mark the position of the middle supports onto the top and bottom shelves with a square and drill 5/32-in. clearance holes through the shelves. Drive 1-5/8-in. screws through the shelf into the supports.

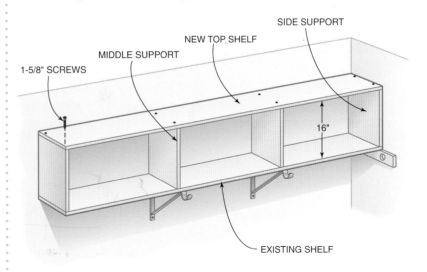

SIDE SUPPORT
NEW TOP SHELF
MIDDLE SUPPORT
1-5/8" SCREWS
16"
EXISTING SHELF

Screw a wire closet shelf to the underside of joists to create a shelf that's strong, easy to see through and won't collect dust.

Joist-space space-saver

Don't waste all that space between joists in a basement or garage. Screw wire shelving to the underside of the joists. An 8-ft. x 16-in. length of wire shelving and a pack of plastic clips (sold separately) will take only 15 minutes to install.

Shoe-storage booster stool

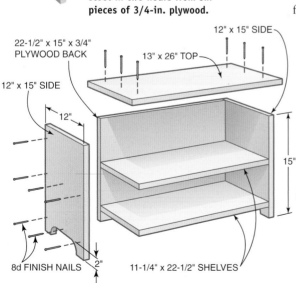

Build this double-duty step stool in two hours from six pieces of 3/4-in. plywood.

Build this handy stool in two hours and park it in your closet. You can also use it as a step to reach the high shelf. All you need is a 4x4 sheet of 3/4-in. plywood, wood glue and a handful of 8d finish nails. Cut the plywood pieces according to the illustration. Spread wood glue on the joints, then nail them together with 8d finish nails. First nail through the sides into the back. Then nail through the top into the sides and back. Finally, mark the location of the two shelves and nail through the sides into the shelves.

22-1/2" x 15" x 3/4" PLYWOOD BACK

12" x 15" SIDE

13" x 26" TOP

12" x 15" SIDE

12"

15"

8d FINISH NAILS

2"

11-1/4" x 22-1/2" SHELVES

Closet nook shelves

Salvage the hidden space at the recessed ends of your closets by adding a set of shelves. Wire shelves are available in a variety of widths at home centers. Measure the width and depth of the space. Then choose the correct shelving and ask the salesperson to cut the shelves to length for you. Subtract 3/8 in. from the actual width to determine the shelf length. Buy a pair of end mounting brackets and a pair of plastic clips for each shelf.

Make the most of the recesses at the ends of your closet with wire shelving.

tip **Double-duty luggage**
Put your luggage to use when it's not on vacation. Fill it with off-season clothes and stash it under the bed.

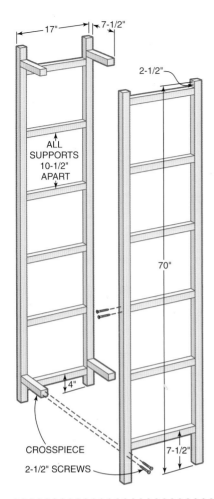

Stacked recycling tower

Five plastic containers, six 2x2s and screws, and one hour's work are all it takes to put together this space-saving recycling storage rack. Our frame fits containers that have a top that measures 14-1/2 in. x 10 in. and are 15 in. tall. The containers shown were made by Rubbermaid.

If you use different-size containers, adjust the distance between the uprights so the 2x2s will catch the lip of the container. Then adjust the spacing of the horizontal rungs for a snug fit when the container is angled as shown.

Start by cutting the 2x2s to length according to the illustration. Then mark the position of the rungs on the uprights. Drill two 5/32-in. holes through the uprights at each crosspiece position. Drill from the outside to the inside and angle the holes inward slightly to prevent the screws from breaking out the side of the rungs.

Drive 2-1/2-in. screws through the uprights into the rungs. Assemble the front and back frames. Then connect them with the side crosspieces.

Build a space-saving tower for plastic recycling containers in one hour with simple 2x2 and screw construction.

Cut slots in a piece of plywood with a jigsaw. Fill resealable bags with small parts, hardware or craft items and hang them from the slotted plywood.

Sandwich-bag parts organizer

Keep screws, connectors, nails and other small parts in sight and handy with this resealable bag holder. You can build it in one hour out of a 3/4-in.-thick scrap of plywood. Start by cutting two pieces of plywood as shown. Draw lines 1 in. apart across the shorter piece with a square, stopping 1 in. from the edge. Now cut along the lines with a jigsaw. Screw the two pieces of plywood together and screw the unit to the wall. Fill resealable bags and slip them into the slots.

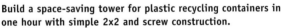

7 *quick* clutter busters

Clever projects to help you cut clutter fast

1 Adjustable spice shelf

This in-cabinet spice shelf puts small containers at eye level and still leaves room in the cabinet for tall items. The materials are inexpensive, and building and installing it will take only an hour or so. You'll need a 4-ft. 1x3 for the top shelf and a 4-ft. 1x2 for the bottom ledger. You can find shelf pegs at home centers in two sizes, 1/4 in. and 3/16 in., so measure the holes in your cabinet before you shop. The secret is to assemble the shelf outside the cabinet and then set it on the shelf pegs.

Measure the sides and back of your cabinet and cut your shelf and ledger pieces. Subtract 1/8 in. from all sides so you can fit the unit into the cabinet. Attach the sides to the back of the bottom ledger and put two nails into each butt joint. Then nail the top shelf sides into place and pin the shelf back at the corners to hold it flush (Photo 1).

To install the shelf unit, carefully fit one end of the "U" into the cabinet, holding it higher at one end, and shimmy it down until it sits firmly on top of the shelf pegs (Photo 2). Shift the pegs up or down to adjust the shelf height. Spray a quick coat of lacquer on the shelf before installing it to make it more scrubbable.

1 Nail the back and side ledgers together, then nail on the side shelves. Measure between the side shelves and cut the back shelf to fit.

2 Set the spice shelf on adjustable shelf pegs. You may have to remove an existing shelf so you can tilt the spice shelf into place.

2 Bathroom shelving unit

In a small bathroom, every single square inch counts. These shelves make the most of wall space by going vertical. The version shown here, made of cherry, cost about $100. But you can build one for half of that or less if you choose a more economical wood like oak or pine. All you need is two hours, a 6-ft. 1x4, a 6-ft. 1x6 and a 6-ft. 1x8.

Cut the middle spacers and the shelves 12 in. long. Cut the bottom spacer 11 in. long to allow for a decorative 1-in. reveal. Cut the top spacer to fit (the one shown is 7-1/4 in.). Measure 1 in. from one edge of the backboard and draw a guideline for the shelves and spacers along its length. Nail the bottom spacer in place, leaving a 1-in. reveal at the bottom edge. Center the first shelf by measuring 3-1/4 in. in from the edge of the backboard and nail it in place. Work your way up the backboard, alternating between spacers and shelves (Photo 1).

On the back side, use a 1/8-in. countersink bit to drill two holes, one at the top and one at the bottom of each spacer. Drill two holes spaced 1 in. from each side of the backboard into each shelf ledge. Drive 1-1/4-in. drywall screws into each hole (Photo 2). Paint or stain the assembled unit. If you'd like to clearcoat it, use a wipe-on poly or spray lacquer—using a brush would be really tough. Mount the unit on the wall with two 2-1/2-in. screws and screw-in drywall anchors (E-Z Ancor is one brand). Drive the screws where they won't be seen: right below the bottom shelf and right above the top shelf.

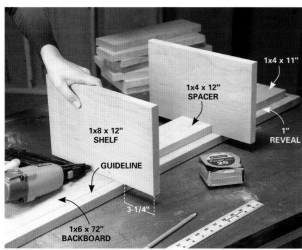

1 Nail the spacers and shelves in place, starting at the bottom and working your way up. Place the bottom spacer 1 in. from the lower edge of the backboard.

2 Strengthen the shelves by driving screws through the backboard into the shelves and spacers. Drill screw holes with a countersink bit.

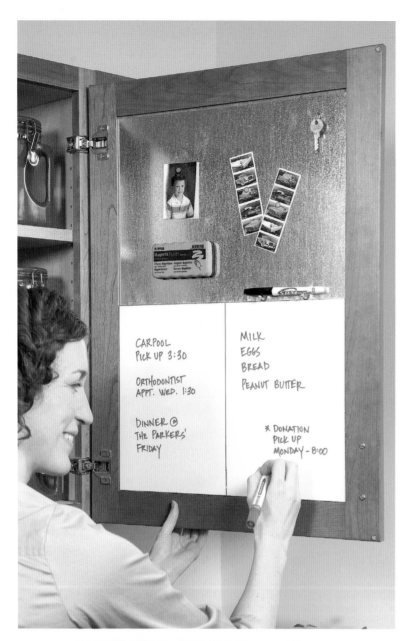

3 Cabinet door message board

A sheet of metal and a dry-erase board can turn any cabinet door into a convenient message center. You'll find 2 x 2-ft. lengths of plastic-coated hardboard (often called "whiteboard" or "dry-erase" board) and sheet metal at a hardware store or home center. Larger hardware stores will cut the sheet metal to your specifications. Be sure to get steel instead of aluminum so magnets will stick. Including a can of spray adhesive, you'll spend around $20, and your message board will be up and ready to use in one hour!

If you cut the metal yourself, wear gloves to protect your hands and use tin snips carefully. Use a metal file to smooth any ragged edges. If you don't have a table saw to cut the whiteboard, flip it over, mark your measurements and use a jigsaw to cut it from the back to prevent chipping or splintering. To get a straight cut, use a framing square as a guide (Photo 1).

To mount the metal sheet and whiteboard to the inside of the door, take the door off its hinges, lay it flat and carefully mask off the area where you want to spray the adhesive. Follow the directions on the can to apply the adhesive to the door, metal and whiteboard (Photo 2). Mount the pieces, press firmly and let dry.

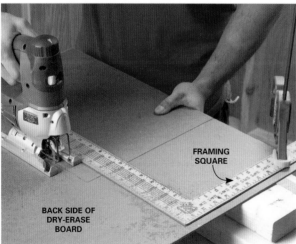

1 Cut the dry-erase board from the back to avoid chipping the plastic-coated face. Use a framing square as a guide to get a straight cut.

2 Spray adhesive onto the door, metal and dry-erase board. Carefully position the metal and board as you stick them to the door—once they're in place, you can't move them.

4 Cutting board rack

You can make this nifty rack for less than $10 and mount it inside a cabinet door to stash your cutting boards out of sight. It goes together in about 15 minutes since it only requires a 6-ft. 1x2 and two L-brackets.

Measure between the door stiles to get the maximum width of your rack. Make sure the rack will be wide enough for your cutting boards (or spring for new ones). You'll also need to mount the rack low enough so it doesn't bump into a cabinet shelf when the door closes. Cut the bottom and face rails to match the space between the cabinet door stiles.

Cut the sides 7-1/4 in. long. Nail the sides to the bottom rail. Then nail the two face pieces at the top and bottom to complete the rack (Photo 1). The easiest way to mount the rack is to take the cabinet door off its hinges and lay it down. Predrill the screw holes for the L-brackets. Mount the rack to the cabinet door using a 1-in. L-bracket on each side of the rack and 1/2-in. wood screws (Photo 2).

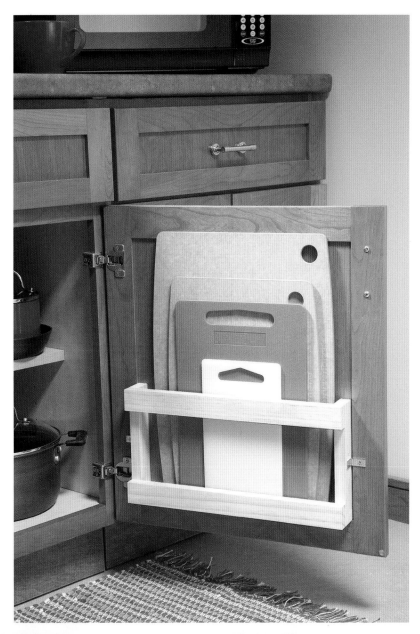

1 Nail the bottom rail to the sides, then nail on the face rails. For a quick, clear finish, spray on two light coats of lacquer.

FACE RAIL

BOTTOM RAIL

FACE RAIL

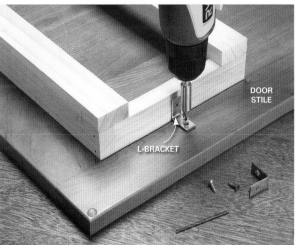

2 Mount the rack on the door with L-brackets. This is easiest if you remove the door. Be sure to predrill screw holes in the door stiles.

DOOR STILE

L-BRACKET

5 Magnetic office supplies holder

If you have an hour to spare, use it to organize all those paper clips, rubber bands
and pushpins. All it takes is a magnetic
knife/tool holder strip, small jars with lids
and a few fender washers. (The strips are
available at bath stores, hardware stores,
home centers and online retailers.) You
don't even need the fender washers if you
buy jars with steel lids that will stick to the
magnet on their own.

Clamp the magnetic strips to the
underside of a shelf or cabinet. Drill pilot
holes and screw the strip into place (Photo
1). If the jars have steel lids, fill them
with office supplies and stick them up
on the magnetic strip. If the jar lids are
aluminum or plastic, use cyanoacrylate
glue (Super Glue is one brand) to attach a
fender washer to the top of each lid (Photo
2). After they dry, fill the jars and stick
them up on the magnet.

tip It's important to keep computer components at least
6 in. away from magnets.

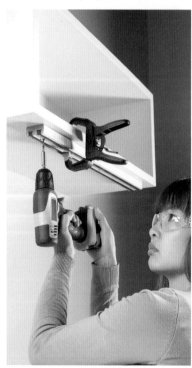

1 Clamp the magnetic strip in place,
drill pilot holes and drive in the
screws that come with the strips.

FENDER
WASHER

2 Glue fender washers to plastic or
aluminum jar lids so they'll stick
to the magnetic strip. Skip this step if
your jars have steel lids.

6 Tie, scarf and belt organizer

Clean up a messy closet by hanging your ties, belts and scarves on this 3-in-1 closet organizer! All you need is a 2 x 2-ft. piece of 1/2-in. plywood, a wooden hanger, a hook (the one shown came from the wooden hanger) and a few hours.

This organizer is 12 in. wide and 16 in. tall, but yours can be taller or narrower. To get a nice curve at the top, use the wooden hanger as a guide. Center it, trace the edge and cut it out with a jigsaw. Make a pattern of holes, slots and notches on a piece of paper and transfer it to your board. Use a 2-in. hole saw to cut the holes, making sure the board is clamped down tightly to keep the veneer from chipping (Photo 1). Use a jigsaw to cut out the side notches. To cut the slots, punch out the ends with a 5/8-in. Forstner drill bit (or a sharp spade bit) to prevent chipping, and then use a jigsaw to finish cutting out the center of each slot (Photo 2).

Sand the hanger and apply several coats of sealer or poly to smooth the edges so your scarves and ties don't snag (this is the most time-consuming step). Using a 1/4-in. round-over bit with a router makes the sanding go faster. Drill a small hole into the top of the hanger for your hook, squeeze in a bit of epoxy glue to hold it and then screw it in.

1 Drill scarf holes with a 2-in. hole saw. Clamp the plywood tightly against a piece of scrap wood to prevent chipping as the hole saw exits the plywood.

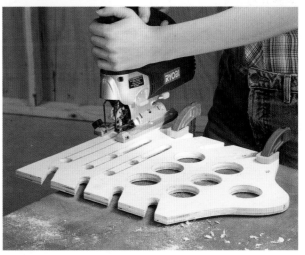

2 Use a 5/8-in. Forstner drill bit or a sharp spade bit to punch out the ends of the slots, and then finish cutting them out with a jigsaw.

7 Laundry room ironing center

To keep your ironing gear handy but out from underfoot, make this simple ironing center in a couple of hours. All you need is a 10-ft. 1x8, a 2-ft. piece of 1x6 for the shelves and a pair of hooks to hang your ironing board.

Cut the back, sides, shelves and top. Align the sides and measure from the bottom 2 in., 14-3/4 in. and 27-1/2 in. to mark the bottom of the shelves (Photo 1). Before assembling the unit, use a jigsaw to cut a 1 x 1-in. dog ear at the bottom of the sides for a decorative touch.

Working on one side at a time, glue and nail the side to the back. Apply glue and drive three 1-5/8-in. nails into each shelf, attach the other side and nail those shelves into place to secure them. Clamps are helpful to hold the unit together while you're driving nails. Center the top piece, leaving a 2-in. overhang on both sides, and glue and nail it into place (Photo 2). Paint or stain the unit and then drill pilot holes into the top face of each side of the unit and screw in the hooks to hold your ironing board. Mount the shelf on drywall using screw-in wall anchors.

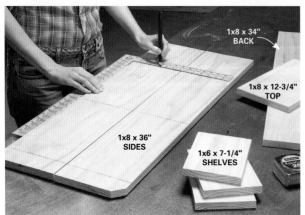

1x8 x 34" BACK
1x8 x 12-3/4" TOP
1x8 x 36" SIDES
1x6 x 7-1/4" SHELVES

1 Place the sides next to each other and mark the shelf positions. For easier finishing, sand all the parts before marking and assembly.

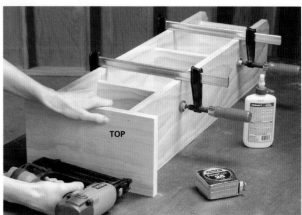

TOP

2 Glue and nail the back and shelves between the sides, then add the top. After painting or staining, screw on hooks for the ironing board.

Simple shoe storage

1 Clamp the 1x3 support to a piece of scrap wood as you drill the holes to prevent the wood from splintering.

6-3/4"
1-3/8" 3-1/2" 3/4" 5/8"
5-1/8"

It doesn't take long for shoes to pile up into a mess next to entry doors. In an hour or so, you can untangle the mess with a simple, attractive shoe ladder that keeps everything from boots to slippers organized and off the floor.

Cut and drill the dowel supports (Photo 1), then screw them to 1x4s (Photo 2). Cut the 1x4s to fit your shoes and the available space—an average pair of adult shoes needs 10 in. of space. Nail or glue the dowels into the dowel supports, leaving 2 in. (or more) extending beyond the supports at the end to hang sandals or slippers.

Apply finish before you mount the shoe ladder to the wall. Screw the shoe ladder to studs or use heavy-duty toggle-bolt style anchors to hold it in place.

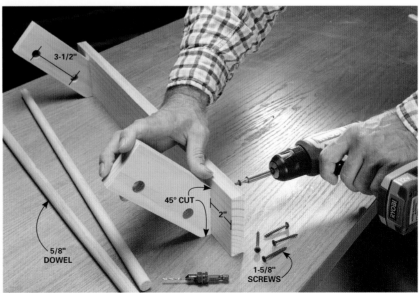

3-1/2"
45° CUT
2"
5/8" DOWEL
1-5/8" SCREWS

2 Predrill through the back of the 1x4 into the 1x3 supports, then glue and screw the pieces together.

Clutter-free laundry room
These fast and easy projects create a pleasant, efficient work area

Closet rod and shelf

This project will save you hours of ironing and organizing. Now you can hang up your shirts and jackets as soon as they're out of the dryer—no more wrinkled shirts at the bottom of the basket. You'll also gain an out-of-the-way upper shelf to store all sorts of odds and ends.

Just go to your home center and get standard closet rod brackets, a closet rod and a precut 12-in.-deep melamine shelf. Also pick up some drywall anchors, or if you have concrete, some plastic anchors and a corresponding masonry bit. Follow the instructions in Photos 1 and 2.

You can get these great-looking Lido Rail chrome brackets and rod at home centers or buy them online.

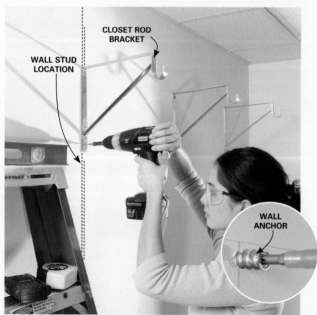

WALL STUD LOCATION

CLOSET ROD BRACKET

WALL ANCHOR

1 Draw a level line about 78 in. above the floor and locate the studs behind the drywall. Fasten at least two of your closet rod brackets into wall studs (4 ft. apart) and then center the middle bracket with two 2-in.-long screws into wall anchors (inset).

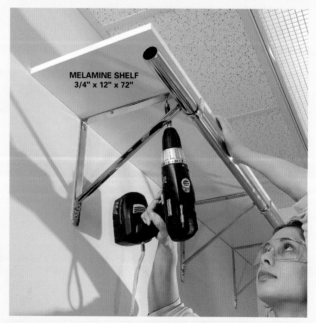

MELAMINE SHELF
3/4" x 12" x 72"

2 Fasten your 12-in.-deep melamine shelf onto the tops of the brackets with 1/2-in. screws. Next, insert your closet rod, drill 1/8-in. holes into the rod, and secure it to the brackets with No. 6 x 1/2-in. sheet metal screws.

1x10 SHELF

1-5/8" SCREW WITH FINISH WASHER

1x3 MOUNTING STRIP SCREWED TO WALL

1x10 SIDE

Simple laundry organizer

Make laundry day easier with this shelf for all your detergents, stain removers and other supplies. Build this simple organizer from 1x10 and 1x3 boards. If you have a basement laundry room, you may need to cut an access through the shelves for your dryer exhaust.

Quick washer and dryer shelf

Clean up the clutter of detergent boxes, bleach bottles and other laundry room stuff. Install a shelf that fits just above the washer and dryer. Screw ordinary shelf brackets to the wall and mount a board that just clears the tops.

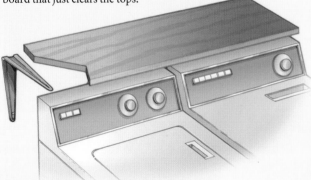

Hanger shelf

Sometimes you just need another place to hang clothes, like on the shelf over your washer and dryer. Turn the edge of that shelf into a hanger rack by predrilling some 3/4-in. plastic pipe and screwing it to the top of the shelf along the edge.

3/4" PLASTIC PIPE

DIY washer/dryer pedestals

Save a bundle by building your own front-loading washer and dryer pedestals. The key is to make the pedestal sturdy, since front-loaders have a tendency to move around if they're not on a solid, level surface.

To start, measure the length and width of your washer and dryer. That's your minimum size for the pedestals. You can make them longer and wider if you want the extra space to stand on to reach overhead shelving or to set the laundry baskets on. Or you can make one long pedestal to fit under both the washer and the dryer (see illustration).

Build the pedestal out of 2x10 or 2x12 lumber. Feel free to add an attractive finish. Use shims to level the pedestal before you set the appliance on it.

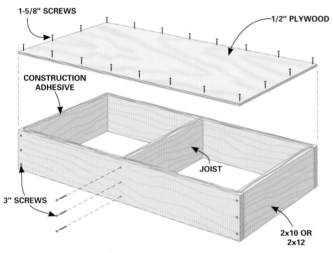

Fasten the frame together with 3-in. screws. Attach a joist in the middle. Apply construction adhesive to eliminate squeaks, then fasten 1/2-in. plywood over the top with 1-5/8-in. screws.

Drying rack

Finally, a great place to dry brushes and other small items in your utility tub. Form a hook in a wire shelf section by hammering one side around a scrap of 2x4. Hang it over the tub's edge for a clever shelf.

Sock stopper

Stuff a strip of foam pipe insulation into the space between your washer and your dryer or along the wall. That way, socks can't slip into the abyss.

Washing hose security

Washing machine discharge hoses can jump out of the laundry tub and flood the entire room. To prevent this, use a 1-1/4-in. hole saw to drill through the fiberglass laundry tub. Pull the discharge hose up through the hole and into the tub.

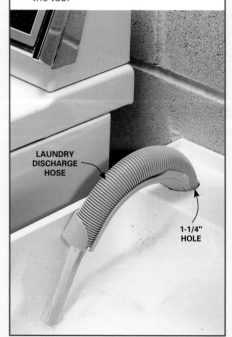

CHAPTER

2 Kitchen & bath upgrades

Kitchens and bathrooms, more so than other rooms in your home, must be hardworking public spaces. You want these rooms to look good, and you need them to function well for you and your family. If you don't have the time or budget for a major kitchen or bathroom remodel right now, here are 18 big-impact improvements you can do in a matter of hours.

Even if you've never tried tiling before, you can update your kitchen backsplash in one weekend. Does your toilet need replacing? It's a snap! It'll take you no more than a couple of hours if you follow the step-by-step instructions that begin on p. 34.

Mosaic backsplash

A whole new look in just two mornings

Nothing packs more style per square inch than mosaic tile. So if your kitchen's got the blahs, give it a quick infusion of pizzazz with a tile backsplash. Because the small tiles are mounted on 12 x 12-in. sheets, installation is fast. You can install the tile on Saturday and then grout it on Sunday.

Professionals charge by the sq. ft. for installing tile (plus materials), so you'll save big by installing it yourself. Tile styles and prices run the gamut from bargain basic to expensive elegance. Shown here are slate tiles, which sometimes crumble when you cut them. Other types of mosaic tile, especially ceramic tiles, are easier to cut.

Here you'll learn how to install tile sheets. You'll need basic tile tools, available at home centers and tile stores, including a 3/16-in. trowel and a grout float. You'll also need mastic adhesive, grout and grout sealer. You can rent a wet saw to cut the tiles.

METALLIC — **GLASS**

Mosaic tile sheets make it easy to achieve a great backsplash. Layout is a cinch—you can simply cut the mesh backing on the sheets to fit the tile along counters and cabinets. In fact, the hardest part of this or any other tiling project may be choosing the look—the tiles come in a variety of shapes and materials, and many sheets have glass or metallic tiles built in for accents. To add to your options, strips of 4 x 12-in. tiles are available for borders. So you can match the existing look of your kitchen— or try something new!

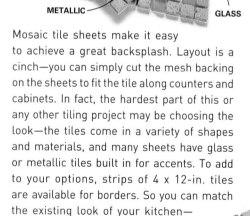

Prepare the walls

Before installing the tile, clean up any grease splatters on the wall (mastic won't adhere to grease). Wipe the stains with a sponge dipped in a mixture of water and mild dishwashing liquid (like Dawn). If you have a lot of stains or they won't come off, wipe on a paint deglosser with a lint-free cloth or abrasive pad so the mastic will adhere. Deglosser is available at paint centers and home centers.

Then mask off the countertops and any upper cabinets that will have tile installed along the side. Leave a 1/4-in. gap between the wall and the tape for the tile (Photo 1). Cover the countertops with newspaper or a drop cloth.

Turn off power to the outlets in the wall and remove the cover plates. Make sure the power is off with a noncontact voltage detector. Place outlet extenders in the outlet boxes. The National Electrical Code requires extenders when the boxes are more than 1/4 in. behind the wall surface. It's easier to put in extenders now and cut tile to fit around them than to add them later if the tile opening isn't big enough. Set the extenders in place as a guide for placing the tile. You'll remove them later for grouting.

On the wall that backs your range, measure down from the top of the countertop backsplash a distance that's equal to three or four full rows of tile (to avoid cutting the tile) and make a mark. Screw a scrap piece of wood (the ledger board) to the wall at the mark between the cabinets.

The area between the range and the vent hood is usually the largest space on the wall—and certainly the most seen by the cooks in the house—so it'll serve as your starting point for installing the tile. Make a centerline on the wall halfway between the cabinets and under the vent hood (Photo 1). Measure from the centerline to the cabinets. If you'll have to cut tile to fit, move the centerline slightly so you'll only have to cut the mesh backing (at least on one side).

Install and seal the tile

Using a 3/16-in. trowel, scoop some mastic adhesive out of the tub and put it on the wall (no technique involved here!). Spread the mastic along the centerline, cutting in along the ledger board, vent hood and upper cabinets (Photo 2). Then use broad strokes to fill in the middle. Hold the trowel at a 45-degree angle to the wall to spread the mastic thin—you should be able to see the layout lines where the points of the trowel touch the wall. Have a water bucket and sponge on hand to keep the trowel clean. Whenever the mastic starts to harden on the trowel, wipe it off with the wet sponge.

Place plastic tile spacers on the ledger board and countertop. This leaves a gap so the tiles don't sit directly on the countertop (you'll caulk the gap later).

Align the first tile sheet with the centerline, directly over the spacers. Press it onto the wall with your hand. If the sheet slides around and mastic comes through the joint lines, you're applying the mastic too thick (remove the sheet, scrape off some mastic and retrowel). Scrape out any mastic in the joints with a utility knife.

Eyeball a 1/16-in. joint between sheets of tile (you don't need spacers). After every two or three installed sheets, tap them into the mastic with a board and rubber mallet (Photo 3).

If tiles fall off the sheets, dab a little mastic on the back and

1 Mark a centerline between the upper cabinets so the tiles will be centered under the vent hood. Screw a ledger board to the wall to support the tile.

2 Spread a thin layer of mastic adhesive on the wall, starting at the centerline. Spread just enough adhesive for two or three sheets at a time so the adhesive doesn't dry before you set the tile.

3 Tap the tile into the mastic with a wood scrap and a rubber mallet. Stand back, look at the tiles and straighten any crooked ones.

SPACER →

4 Cut tile sheets to the nearest full row to fit around outlets, then fill the gaps with tiles cut on a wet saw.

stick them right back in place. The sheets aren't perfectly square, so you may need to move individual tiles to keep joints lined up. Move the tiles with your fingers or by sticking a utility knife blade in the joint and turning the blade. If an entire sheet is crooked, place a grout float over the tile and move the sheet. You'll have about 20 minutes after installing the tile to fine-tune it.

If you're lucky, you can fit the tile sheets under upper cabinets and around outlets by cutting the mesh backing with a utility knife. If not, you'll have to cut the tile with a wet saw. Nippers and grinders cause the slate tiles to shatter or crumble, although you can use these tools on ceramic tile.

Slice the backing to the nearest full row of tile, install the sheet around the outlet or next to the cabinet, then cut tiles with a wet saw to fill the gaps (Photo 4). Cut the tiles while they're attached to the sheet. Individual tiles are too small to cut (the blade can send them flying!).

Let the tile sit for at least 30 minutes, then apply a grout sealer if you're using natural stone (like slate) or unglazed quarry tile. The sealer keeps the grout from sticking to the tile (it's not needed for nonporous tiles such as ceramic). Pour the sealer on a sponge, then wipe on just enough to dampen the tiles.

Grout and clean the tile

Wait 24 hours after installing the tile to add the grout. Use a premium grout that has a consistent color and resists stain. Since the backsplash will be subject to splatters and stains from cooking and food prep, spend the extra money for a premium grout. You can find or special order it at home centers or tile stores. One brand is Prism. Sanded grout will also work and will save you a few bucks.

Mix the grout with water until it reaches mashed potato consistency, then put some on the wall with a grout float. Work the grout into the joints by moving the float diagonally over the tiles (Photo 5). Hold the grout float at a 45-degree angle to the tile. Scrape off excess grout with the float after the joints are filled.

Ten minutes after grouting, wipe the grout off the surface of the tiles with a damp sponge. If the grout pulls out of the joints, wait another 10 minutes for it to harden. Continually rinse the sponge in a bucket of water and wipe the tiles until they're clean.

These slate tiles have a lot of crevices that retain grout. While most of the grout comes off the tiles with the wet sponge, some won't. Most pro installers leave some grout in slate and other rough-surface tile—it's just part of the deal with some types of natural stone. But if you want the tile completely clean, remove the grout from individual tiles with a toothbrush.

After cleaning the wall, use a utility knife to rake the grout out of the joints along the bottom of the backsplash and in the inside corners (Photo 6). These expansion joints allow the wall to move without cracking the grout.

Two hours after grouting, wipe the haze off the tiles with microfiber cloths. Then caulk the expansion joints with latex caulk. Use a colored caulk that closely matches the grout.

After seven days, sponge on a grout sealer to protect the grout against stains.

That's it! Now every time your family and friends gather in your kitchen, they'll be impressed with your custom backsplash.

5 Force grout into the joints with a float. Scrape off excess grout by moving the float diagonally across the tile.

DULL SIDE

6 Rake the grout out of the joints at inside corners and along the bottom with a utility knife so you can fill them with caulk. Keep the dull side of the blade along the countertop.

Add under-cabinet lights

Good lighting allows you to make the best use of the space you have. Dimly lit or shadowy countertops are hard to work at. Adding undercabinet lights is a great way to make the countertops more useful while making a small kitchen feel larger.

It's easy to wire for undercabinet lights with the rest of the wiring during a kitchen remodel. But adding them to an existing kitchen requires a little more ingenuity. Visit familyhandyman.com and search "under cabinet lighting" for step-by-step how-to. Otherwise, you can fish the electrical cables through the basement, crawlspace or attic and pull them through the stud spaces to each light fixture. As a last resort, buy plug-in type undercabinet lights.

Two-hour glass cabinet doors

A pair of glass doors can add a designer touch to any kitchen. They can turn an ordinary cabinet into a decorative showcase or simply break up an otherwise monotonous row of solid doors. This alteration works only for frame-and-panel cabinet doors (see Figure A), where you can replace the inset wood panels with glass. Converting the two doors shown here took about two hours.

To get started, remove the doors from the cabinets and remove all hardware from the doors. Examine the back side of each door; you might find a few tiny nails where the panel meets the frame. If so, gouge away wood with a utility knife to expose the nail heads and pull the nails with a pliers. Look carefully; just one leftover nail will chip your expensive router bit.

Cut away the lips using a router and a 1/2-in. pattern bit (Photo 1). A pattern bit is simply a straight bit equipped with a bearing that rolls along a guide. Most home centers and hardware stores don't carry pattern bits, but they are readily available online. Be sure to choose a bit that has the bearing on the top, not at the bottom.

Use any straight, smooth material (solid wood, plywood or MDF) to make two 3-1/2-in.-wide guides. To allow for the 1-in. cutting depth of our pattern bit, we nailed layers of plywood and MDF together to make 1-3/8-in. thick guides. Position the guides 1/2 in. from the inner edges of the lips and clamp them firmly in place over the door. Support the outer edges of the guides with strips of wood that match the thickness of the door to keep them level (Photo 1). Before you start routing, make sure the door itself is clamped firmly in place.

Set the router on the guide and adjust the cutting depth so that the bit just touches the panel. Cut away the lips on two sides, then reposition the guides to cut away the other two. With the lips removed, lift

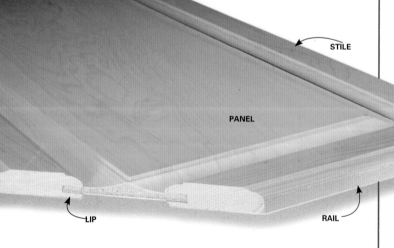

Figure A Panel door profile

Most cabinet doors are made like this one: A raised or flat panel fits into grooves in the rails-and-stile frame. To remove the panel, just cut away the lips on the back side of the door.

1 Clamp router guides to the back side of the door. Run a pattern bit along the guides to cut away the inside lips.

PATTERN BIT

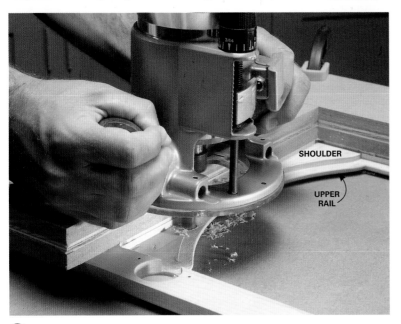

2 Lower the router bit and cut away the shoulders on the back side of an arched upper rail to create a square recess for the glass.

3 Set the glass into the frame and secure it with glass clips placed no more than 12 in. apart. Then reinstall the doors.

the panel out of the frame. If the panel is stuck, a few light hammer taps will free it.

If your door frame has a rectangular opening, it's now ready for glass. If it has an arched upper rail, cut a square recess above the arch (Photo 2). This allows you to use a rectangular piece of glass rather than a curved piece (curved cuts are expensive). Then simply lay the glass in and anchor it with glass clips (Photo 3). Clips are usually available from the glass supplier.

If the glass rattles in the frame, add pea-size blobs of hot-melt glue every 12 in.

GLASS CLIPS

Buying glass

Most hardware stores carry clear glass and will cut it for free or a small fee. Ask for 3/16-in.-thick "double strength" glass. Order glass panels 1/8 in. smaller than the recess in the frame. To find tempered, textured or colored glass, do a search online for "glass." We bought clear textured glass and paid the supplier extra to have the two panels tempered. Building codes require tempered glass for locations within 5 ft. of the floor.

Kitchen & bath spruce-ups

Quick DIY floating tile floor

The SnapStone system makes laying tile so simple. Each 12-in. porcelain tile has a plastic backing that interlocks with the backing on other tiles. The snapped-together tile surface "floats" over subfloors, concrete, vinyl or existing wood floors. Installation goes quick because there's no need to install special underlayments, mix adhesives or even worry about precise tile spacing. Make any cuts with a tile saw just as you would with ordinary tile. But since it's not firmly adhered to the floor, you can't use ordinary grout; it's too brittle. Instead, the manufacturer offers a special flexible grout that will flex with any floor movement without cracking. (A 1-gallon pail covers up to 65 sq. ft.) Or you can choose snap-in grout-line strips.

SnapStone is available in many colors and tile sizes.

snapstone.com

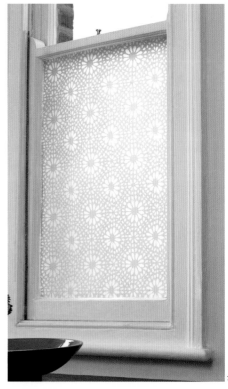

SPECIAL FLEXIBLE GROUT

INTERLOCKING EDGE

30-minute lace curtain window film

This decorative adhesive window film installs in minutes, provides privacy and still lets the sunshine in. Available in six different patterns, the film is applied to the glass. You simply wipe the glass with water, remove the backing and apply the film. It adheres well, yet can be removed easily with a scraper without leaving a residue. The all-over pattern means you can hang the film vertically or horizontally, and the grid on the backing paper makes it easy to cut and measure. The film works on any glass surface, including mirrors, cabinet doors and tables. A 37 x 52-in. roll is available from 2jane.

2jane.com

Tin backsplash or ceilings, made easy

Armstrong's Metallaire decorative metal ceiling and backsplash tiles can create an air of elegance in any room. Installing a backsplash in an average-size kitchen will take a morning.

The backsplash and wall tiles are available in 18 x 48-in. panels in five styles with a stainless steel finish. The ceiling tiles come in 12 stamped metal patterns (including Vine and Medallion) and five finishes—steel, chrome, brass, copper and paint-able white. The 2 x 4-ft. ceiling tiles can be nailed directly to plywood or furring strips, and the 2 x 2-ft. ceiling tiles can be used with a suspended grid system that has the same finish as the tiles. Six cornice designs are also available. armstrong.com

Armstrong's Metallaire product line features 12 styles of decorative metal ceiling tiles, six cornices and five backsplash tile patterns in a variety of finishes.

Four-hour roll-on stainless steel

Apply Liquid Stainless Steel to your kitchen appliances and you'll have the stainless steel look without having to buy new (it's great for giving aging appliances a face-lift!). The water-based latex paint is made with stainless steel and applied with foam brushes and a roller (included with paint purchase). A topcoat gives the surface a durable satin or gloss finish (your choice).

The paint can be used on stoves, refrigerators, dishwashers and toasters—just clean them, tape off areas you don't want covered and start painting. You can apply both coats and the satin or gloss topcoat in a morning. The paint can also be used on kitchen cabinets, tables and chairs (after priming). A Fridge Kit has everything you need to paint your refrigerator. Retailers are listed online, or buy the products directly from the manufacturer.

liquidstainlesssteel.com

Easy-to-install shower seat

A shower seat is a key component for making a bathroom safer for older adults. The one shown here, the Goof Proof Shower Seat by Mark E Industries, can be installed before the tile is installed or retrofitted over the existing tile. The molded plastic seat has built-in level vials to achieve the perfect slope for water drainage, and the kit comes with all the screws, shims and anchors you'll need to finish the job. The seat is 30 in. wide but can be trimmed to 24 in., and it has a capacity of 400 lbs. Look for it at home centers.

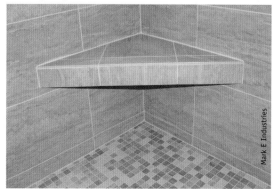

Faster peel-and-stick

Installing new contact paper can be really frustrating as you struggle to separate the contact paper from its backing. To solve the problem, put a piece of tape on one corner of the contact paper, and another piece on the same corner of the backing. Fold down the top of each piece of tape about 1/2 in. to get a better grip, and pull the pieces of tape apart. The paper and backing will separate easily. This also works great on labels, stickers and the like.

Quick counter-top gap filler

If crumbs, papers or even flatware falls into the gap between your countertop and refrigerator, fill the void with nearly invisible plastic tubing. Clear tubing is available at home centers in several widths starting at 1/8 in.

Under-cabinet cleanup

When the floor of your sink cabinet needs a spruce-up, simply lay down squares of self-adhesive vinyl tile. They're about a buck a square at home centers, provide an easy-to-wipe surface and take just minutes to install.

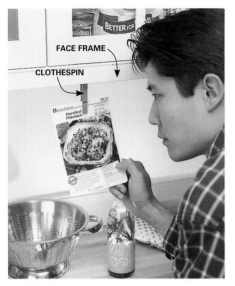

FACE FRAME

CLOTHESPIN

Hide-away hanger

Here's a great way to free up some counter space in a jiffy. Hang recipes from a clothespin mounted with a screw behind your cabinet's face frame. To hide the hanger, just swing it up behind the lip of the frame.

One-hour wine glass molding

T-molding designed for wood floor transitions makes a perfect rack for stemware. Just cut it to length, predrill screw holes and screw it to the underside of a shelf. For a neater look, use brass screws and finish washers. Prefinished T-molding is available wherever wood flooring is sold.

T-MOLDING

FINISH WASHER

Cabinet handle jig

Make quick work of accurately installing new cabinet doors with a jig made from a 4 x 7-in. plywood scrap. Nail a piece of 1x2 over two ends of the plywood. Mark the handle screw locations on the jig and drill guide holes. Now you can screw perfectly placed holes for each door handle in each door. This works great for both two-hole and one-hole handles.

JIG

DOOR HANDLE

Replace a toilet

Tips for a fast, trouble-free, leak-free installation

Whether you're installing a better-flushing toilet or resetting the old one after repairs or remodeling, these tips will help you do it faster and with fewer problems. The job can take less than an hour, but set aside a whole morning in case you run into trouble. Everything you'll need is available at home centers and hardware stores.

Hiring a plumber to replace a toilet typically costs more than $100. If there are hidden problems, such as a broken floor flange, that cost can easily double.

Check the "rough-in"

If you're buying a new toilet, you need to know the "rough-in" measurement of the old one. For the vast majority of toilets, the waste pipe is centered about 12 in. from the wall. But with a few models, that measurement is 10 in. or 14 in. To check the rough-in, just measure from the wall to the toilet's hold-down bolts. If that measurement (plus the thickness of the baseboard) isn't approximately 12 in., toilet shopping will be a bit harder. Most home centers carry only one or two 10-in. models and no 14-in. models. If you have to special-order a toilet, be prepared to spend much more.

If there's a door near the toilet, also measure how far the bowl protrudes from the wall. If you replace a standard bowl with an "elongated" model, the door may not close.

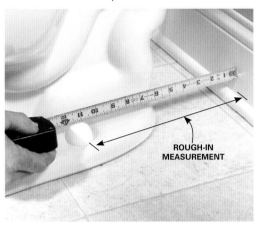

ROUGH-IN MEASUREMENT

Brass bolts are best

Some metal toilet bolts have a yellowish zinc coating that makes them look like brass. So check the label and make sure you're getting brass bolts and nuts. They won't rust away and they're easier to cut off later. If you need to re-anchor the toilet flange, buy stainless steel screws. They won't corrode like steel or break off like brass while you're driving them.

Cut hold-down bolts

Don't be surprised if the old nuts that hold the toilet in place won't budge. Years of corrosion can weld them to their bolts. In that case, a hacksaw blade is the solution. You can buy a "close quarters" blade holder for about $6 at home centers and hardware stores, or just wrap a bare blade with a rag or duct tape. Most toilet bolts and nuts are brass, so they're easy to cut. If the bolt spins, grab it with locking pliers as you cut.

EXTRA NUT AND WASHER

Lock down the bolts

Setting a toilet onto the new bolts can be the most frustrating part of the whole installation. The bolts slip and tip as you're straining to align them with the holes in the toilet. And each time you miss, you risk crushing or shifting the wax ring. The plastic slip-on washers sometimes included with bolts help, but they still allow the bolts to move. The best approach is to buy a second set of nuts and washers so you can lock the bolts in place before you set the toilet. To make sure they're in the correct position, set the toilet and check its height and position. Then lift it off and add the wax ring. To make the bolts easier to find, mark their locations with masking tape.

Flange fixes

A rock-solid toilet flange is the key to a leak-free toilet. The flange is the only thing anchoring the toilet to the floor. If the flange is loose or damaged, the toilet will rock. And a rocking toilet will distort the wax ring and cause leaks. So be sure to scrape off the old wax ring and inspect the flange. Here are some solutions for broken, corroded or loose flanges:

Ear-type ring

Loose flanges are usually the result of wood rot. The flange screws simply won't hold in the soft, decayed subfloor. The best solution depends on the extent of the rot. If the rot is only under the flange, use an ear-type repair ring. The ears let you drive screws into firm wood farther away from the flange. Before you install this kind of ring, hold it up to the drain horn on the underside of the toilet. You may have to cut off a couple of ears to make it work with your toilet. If the rot extends well beyond the flange, you'll have to replace a section of the subfloor.

Repair ring

Plastic flanges often bend or break, but that's an easy fix. Just screw a stainless steel repair ring over the plastic flange with at least four 1-1/2-in. stainless steel screws. Consider doing this even if the plastic flange is in good shape—it's cheap insurance against future trouble. The repair ring raises the flange by about 1/4 in. So before you install the ring, set it on the flange and set your toilet over it to make sure it fits.

Two-part repair ring

Steel flanges attached to plastic hubs can rust away. The easiest solution is a two-part ring that locks onto the plastic just like the old one. To cut away the old flange, use a hacksaw blade or an angle grinder with a metal-cutting wheel. The repair flange is available at some Lowe's stores. To buy online, search for "bay flange."

Repair flange

Cast iron flanges can break or corrode. If only the bolt slot is damaged, slip a repair bracket under the flange. If the flange is in bad shape, you can add a brass repair ring similar to the stainless steel ring shown above or install a plastic flange that slips inside. If necessary, break away the cast iron flange with a cold chisel. Home centers carry one or two slip-in flanges. For a wider variety, search online for "replacement toilet flange."

REPAIR BRACKET

Eliminate rocking with shims

A toilet that rocks on an uneven floor will eventually break the wax ring seal and leak. So check for wobbles after you've set the toilet in place and loosely tightened the nuts. For slight wobbles, slip coins or stainless steel washers into the gaps under the toilet. Don't use regular steel washers, which might rust and stain the floor. For larger gaps, use shims. There are plastic shims made especially for toilets, but plastic construction shims like the ones shown here work just as well. When you've eliminated the wobble, tighten the nuts, cut off the shims and caulk around the toilet base. A toilet set on thick vinyl flooring can loosen as the vinyl compresses. In that case, just retighten the nuts a few days after installation.

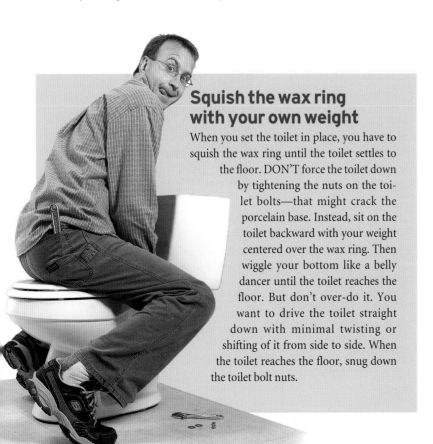

Squish the wax ring with your own weight

When you set the toilet in place, you have to squish the wax ring until the toilet settles to the floor. DON'T force the toilet down by tightening the nuts on the toilet bolts—that might crack the porcelain base. Instead, sit on the toilet backward with your weight centered over the wax ring. Then wiggle your bottom like a belly dancer until the toilet reaches the floor. But don't over-do it. You want to drive the toilet straight down with minimal twisting or shifting of it from side to side. When the toilet reaches the floor, snug down the toilet bolt nuts.

Cut the bolts last

To make positioning a toilet easier, new toilet bolts are extra long. That means you have to cut off the protruding ends later with a hacksaw. But first connect the water line, flush the toilet a couple of times and check for leaks. Leaving the bolts uncut until you've done these final checks lets you easily remove and reset the toilet if you find any problems.

After cutting, double-check the bolts for tightness. Cutting often loosens the nuts a bit.

Don't overtighten the water connections

Do yourself a favor and buy a flexible water supply line. They're a lot easier to install than stiff metal or plastic tubing. Be sure to get one that's covered with stainless steel mesh. For a good seal, hold the hose so it aims straight into the shutoff or fill valve while you're screwing on the connectors. Make them hand-tight, then add another quarter turn with pliers. Connections that are too tight can actually cause leaks or spin the fill valve inside the tank. Check for leaks and tighten them a bit more if needed.

1 Mark the position of the magnets and glue them on the mounting strip, orienting the magnets so they attract each other.

GEL-TYPE SUPER GLUE

12"

4-1/2" MINIMUM

2 Glue the mounting strip to the wall with Super Glue, hot-melt glue or silicone caulk.

Magnetic
toothbrush holder

The problem: Battery-powered toothbrushes don't fit in toothbrush holders and end up lying on a wet, messy countertop.

The solution: Mount neodymium ("rare earth") magnets on a Corian mounting strip with Super Glue. Glue the strip to the wall with Super Glue or silicone caulk.

Tools and materials: To make the mounting strip, cut a Corian threshold with a miter saw or jigsaw. Neodymium magnets are available online. We used 2-in. x 1/2-in. x 1/8-in. magnets. You can double them up if you need more holding power.

Note: Neodymium magnets are incredibly strong but break if handled roughly. Order several more than you need—shipping is expensive. Also, don't handle neodymium magnets if you wear a pacemaker, and never leave them next to your computer.

Make any toothbrush stick

Battery-powered toothbrushes have hidden steel parts that stick to magnets. Mount standard toothbrushes by adding a tiny screw or metal washer to the back.

NO. 4 x 3/8" SCREW

One-morning
medicine cabinet

Clear off your bathroom vanity with a medicine cabinet that tucks inside the wall.

The biggest challenge in installing a recessed cabinet is finding unobstructed stud cavities in an open wall. The wall behind the door is usually open, but make sure that pipes, ducts and wiring don't get in the way. To choose the location for the cabinet, begin by finding the studs with a stud finder. Hold the cabinet to the wall at the best height and mark the cabinet near one side of a stud.

Find the exact location of that stud by sawing through the drywall until the blade is stopped (Photo 1). Use the cuts to define one cabinet side, and draw the cabinet outline.

Cut out the drywall and then cut off the exposed stud (Photo 2). Add the framing, then screw the cabinet to the framing (Photo 5). Add trim around the edges if necessary to conceal the rough drywall edges.

tip Before you cut a full-size hole in the wall, cut a 6 x 6-in. hole and shine a flashlight inside to check for obstructions.

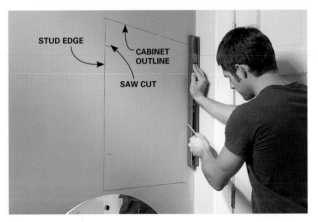

STUD EDGE

CABINET OUTLINE

SAW CUT

1 Outline the inset medicine chest to fall against a stud on one side and cut out the opening with a drywall saw.

2 Cut the intermediate stud flush with the drywall on the back side. Push it sideways to release the drywall screws on the back side and remove the stud.

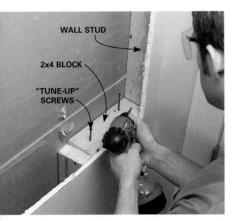

WALL STUD

2x4 BLOCK

"TUNE-UP" SCREWS

3 Screw blocking to adjacent studs at the top and bottom of the opening. Drive temporary "tune-up" screws into the block to help position it.

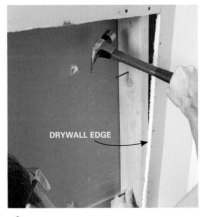

DRYWALL EDGE

4 Cut and tap in vertical backing flush with the drywall edge, then toe-screw it to the blocking.

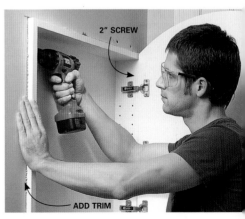

2" SCREW

ADD TRIM

5 Slip the cabinet into the opening and anchor it with pairs of 2-in. screws. Add trim if needed.

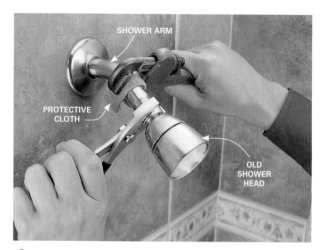

1 Remove your old shower head with pliers. Use a small wrench or another pliers to keep the shower arm from turning. Pad the wrench teeth with a folded piece of cloth so they won't mar the shower arm.

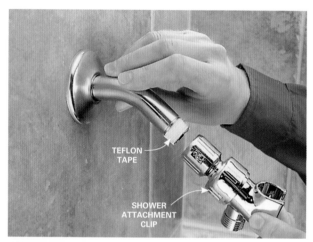

2 Mount the shower attachment clip to the shower arm after cleaning off the old threads and wrapping them (clockwise) with Teflon plumber's tape. Tighten with pliers, using a folded cloth to protect the finish.

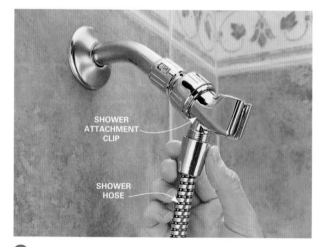

3 Screw the shower hose to the attachment clip and tighten with pliers. In most cases, you won't need Teflon tape on these threads, but check the instructions that came with your new shower head.

Upgrade your
shower
head
today

A detachable hand-held shower head with an adjustable, pulsating spray gives you the luxury of all-over-the-body water massage, plus it's great for washing the kids, the dog and the tub and shower walls. The new head simply screws on in place of the old.

3

Landscaping & backyard projects

Outdoor spaces can often be greatly improved with minor enhancements. And by making your yard more beautiful and accessible, you add precious living space. The One-Day Deck can be built on any flat spot in your yard and promises to be a welcome oasis. Or maybe what your yard needs is a charming, simple path (starting on p. 51).

If you love the look and sounds of water, check out the Special Section of afternoon ponds, fountains and gardens. You may be surprised how easy and inexpensive it is to add a water feature to your landscape.

SPECIAL SECTION:
Afternoon ponds, fountains & gardens

7 one-hour projects

1 Chimney flue planters

Want unique, tough terra cotta planters? Go to a brick supplier and buy 3-ft. lengths of clay chimney flue liner. Cut them to different heights using a circular saw fitted with a masonry cutting blade. Each blade will cut about two liners before wearing out.

The possibilities are endless: You can put the liners on a deck or patio to make a patio garden or accent your landscaping wherever you like—just pick your spots and bury the ends in the soil a little. Group the liners for an elegant herb garden or use them to border landscaped stairs.

Fill the liners with gravel for drainage, leaving at least 8 in. at the top for potting soil. Because the water can drain, the liners won't crack if they freeze. Or simply set plastic pots right on top of the gravel and you'll be able to bring in the plants for the winter.

2 Moss-covered pots

If you like the soft, weathered look of moss-covered pots but don't feel like leaving the process to the whims of nature, try this trick. Search cool, shady spots for moss and gather two or three cups. Put equal parts moss and buttermilk in your blender and mix it up to make a moss milkshake. Paint the moss solution onto any porous, unglazed masonry pot or planter. Place the pot in a shady spot and keep it moist by misting once or twice a day. Depending on the temperature and humidity, you'll start to see moss growing in a month or two. You don't have to wait to add a shade-loving plant to the pot.

MOSS MILKSHAKE

50/50 MOSS AND BUTTERMILK

CONCRETE POT

MIST FREQUENTLY

3 Homemade flower pots

Hypertufa sounds like a high-energy health food, but it's not. It's a concrete-like mixture that contains organic material like peat instead of stones. The peat provides a home in the hardened mix for small plant life such as moss, algae or lichen. When finished and watered, hypertufa looks like an old weathered stone pot. Here's how you can create one:

HYPERTUFA FLOWER POT

1 Buy a plastic milk crate and wrap the sides with chicken wire inside and out. Cut the chicken wire to fit with tin snips. (Be sure to wear gloves; this stuff is sharp!) Use twist ties to secure the wire to the crate.

2 Make up the hypertufa mixture. Combine one part masonry cement, one part sharp sand and one to two parts dry peat. Mix the ingredients thoroughly in a wheelbarrow or 5-gallon bucket. Next, slowly add water while mixing to create a stiff mortar (about the consistency of refrigerated peanut butter).

PEAT
CEMENT
SAND

3 Press the mortar firmly into the chicken wire inside and out until the two layers of the mortar meld to form one. Continue around the pot, covering all four sides. Be sure to wear rubber gloves when working with the mixture because cement can burn your skin. Smooth the surface with your gloves as you work.

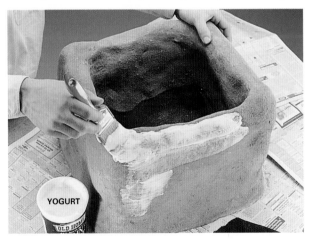

YOGURT

4 Allow the mortar to harden (usually two or three days), then paint the surface with yogurt to encourage the growth of algae. This will give the pot that aged appearance. Finally, place landscape fabric in the bottom and fill the pot with potting soil. Plant the pot with herbs, annuals or perennials.

4 Rot-proof window box

You can't beat the look of a real wood window box on a home. Wood takes paint well, so you can tailor the box's color scheme to complement your house. But ordinary wooden boxes rot out in just a few years, and plastic window boxes won't rot but don't look as nice as the traditional wood box.

This window box design incorporates the best of both materials. Buy a plastic window box at a home or garden center, then construct a cedar frame around it. Size the frame so the lip of the plastic window box rests on the wood. There's no need for

a bottom. Cut the front side of each end piece at a 5-degree angle, then screw together the frame with 2-in. deck screws. Attach the box to the house with a pair of L-brackets, and you're ready to get growing.

5 Easy as 1-2-3 basket

Add pizzazz to your patio, deck or tabletop with this easy-to-make patriotic centerpiece. When the party's over, transplant the annuals into a flower bed or container for a blast of color all summer long.

1. Protect your basket's interior (and your tabletop) by lining it with a piece of plastic or a garbage bag. Be sure it's large enough to fit against the inside walls.

2. Since the plants stay in their original containers, you don't even need to fill the basket with potting soil. Place the tallest plants in the center or back of the basket first. This keeps them from hiding the shorter ones and gives you something to work around. Continue by adding red, white or blue annuals in a pleasing arrangement. Fill in the gaps with ivy, and hide plant pot edges with moss.

3. Dress up your basket with patriotic decorations, such as sparkling floral picks, miniature flags, sparklers or bows.

Materials list

1	4- to 6-in.-deep basket
	Plastic lining or a garbage bag
	Patriotic decorations
1 pkg.	Moss
1	4-in. potted spike
2	4-in. potted ivy plants
3 or 4	4-in. potted red, white or blue annuals

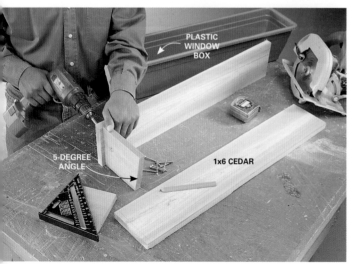

PLASTIC WINDOW BOX

5-DEGREE ANGLE

1x6 CEDAR

6 Space-saving tomatoes

If you're short on space and want to grow tomatoes in pots, you can train them to grow upward like a vine instead of sprawling all over. Make sure you don't buy the bush-type "determinate" tomato, which won't get tall enough to be trained as a vine. "Indeterminate" plants are later maturing, but they will continue to grow and branch until the growing tip (central leader) is cut off. If the label on the plant doesn't say which type of plant you're buying, ask the salesperson.

tip Tomatoes need lots of food and water, but even more so when you grow them in pots.

Buy a roomy pot so roots can spread out and the soil won't dry out too quickly. (The 24-in.-diameter plastic tubs that hold young trees at the nursery are ideal, although 12- to 24-in. pots will do.) You'll need five 6-ft.-long by 3/4-in.-diameter bamboo stakes. Cut one of them into 12-in. lengths. Tie these pieces with twine to the nodules on the vertical stakes, like rungs on a ladder. Push one end of each trellis 1 ft. deep into the pot, placing one trellis in front of the tomato plant and the other behind it.

To train the plant to grow upward like a vine, wind the stems through the trellis and secure with twine. Pinch out some of the side shoots to encourage growth of the central leader.

CENTRAL LEADER

SIDE SHOOT

GARDEN TWINE

BAMBOO STAKES

12" TO 24"-POT

7 Thyme in a stone patio

If you're planning to lay a flagstone or brick patio, leave spaces between the stones for thyme. It creates soft, subtly hued mats that visually soften the stone and release a wonderful fragrance when you step on them. Buy the types that grow well in your region. Space the plants 6 in. apart and let them fill in naturally.

LEMON THYME

WOOLLY THYME

CREEPING THYME

CREEPING THYME

One-day
island deck

Create a comfortable retreat anywhere in your yard

Most decks are attached to houses, but there's no reason they have to be. Sometimes the best spot to set up a deck chair and relax is at the other end of the yard, tucked into a shady corner of the garden. And if you don't attach the deck to the house, you don't need deep frost footings—which can save hours of backbreaking labor, especially in wooded or rocky areas where footings are difficult to dig.

This deck was designed with simple construction in mind. If you can cut boards and drive screws, you can build it. The only power tools you'll need are a circular saw and a drill. Shown is a premium grade of low-maintenance composite decking with

hidden fasteners. Using standard treated decking and screws would lower the cost by about half. You may need to special-order composite decking and hidden fasteners if you use the same types as those shown, but everything else is stocked at home centers or lumberyards.

A few cautions: If all or part of the deck is higher than 30 in. off the ground, you'll need a building permit and railings. If you intend to build any kind of structure on top of the deck or attach the deck to the house, you also need a permit. If you dig footings, call 811 first to check for underground utilities. Also, keep the deck at least 4 ft. back from the property line.

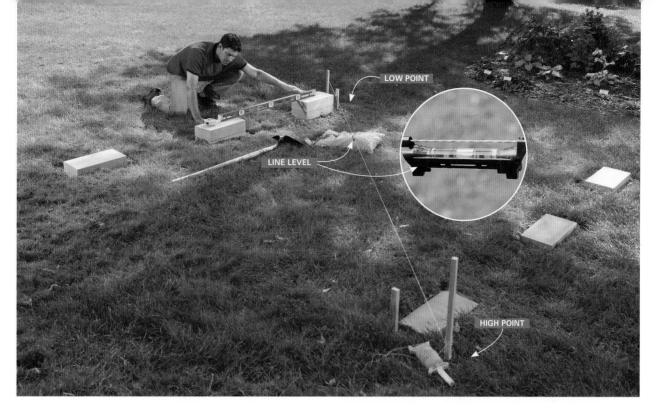

LOW POINT

LINE LEVEL

HIGH POINT

Place the footings and beams

Lay out the two beams parallel to each other, 9 ft. apart. Screw on temporary 1x4 stretchers across the ends of the beams, overhanging them each the same distance, then measure diagonally to make sure the beams are square to each other. Mark the location of the gravel pads (see Figure A) by cutting the grass with a shovel, then move the beams out of the way and cut out the sod where the gravel will go.

Establish the highest and lowest points with a string and string level to get a rough idea of how deep to dig and how much gravel to put in to make the blocks level (Figure A). Tamp the dirt with a block to make a firm base, then spread the gravel. Place the blocks and level them against each other and in both directions (Photo 1), adding or scraping out gravel as needed. Use construction adhesive between the 4-in.-thick blocks if you stack them, or use 8-in. blocks. If your site slopes so much that one side will be more than 2 ft. off the ground, support it on a 4x4 post on a frost footing instead—it'll look better and be safer.

Set the beams across the blocks and square them to each other, using the same 1x4 stretchers to hold them parallel and square (Photo 2). If the beams are not perfectly level, shim them with plastic or pressure-treated wood shims (sold in home centers).

Mark the joist locations on the beams, starting with a joist on the end of each beam. Shown are 11 joists spaced 12 in. on center to keep the composite decking from sagging over time, but wood decking can be spaced 16 in. on center.

1 Lay a quick foundation with minimal digging by setting concrete blocks on gravel. Level from high to low spots in the yard with a string level.

Instead of toenailing, which often splits the wood, use metal angles to hold down the joists. This also makes it easy to place the joists. Attach one alongside each joist location (Photo 3).

Cantilever the joists on all sides

Set the two outer joists and the center joist on the beams against the metal angles. Extend the joists over the beam on one side by 10-1/2 in., but let them run long over the opposite beam. Trim them to exact length when the deck is almost done so you can avoid ripping the last deck board.

Fasten the joists to the angles with deck screws. Screw on both rim joists—you'll have to take the second rim joist back off when the joists are trimmed and then reattach it, but it's needed to hold

A deck you can build in a day

The simplicity of this deck makes it fast to build. With a helper and all the materials ready to go first thing in the morning, you can have a completed deck before sundown. If you add a step to your deck and use hidden deck fasteners as shown here, you might need a few more hours to finish the job.

Figure A
Island deck

Dimensions:
11' 8" square (not including stairs)

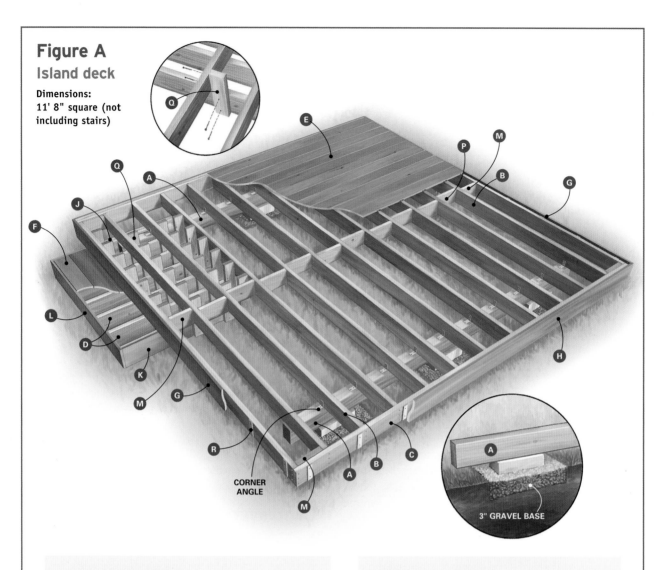

CORNER ANGLE

3" GRAVEL BASE

Materials list

ITEM	QTY.
4" x 8" x 12" solid concrete block	6 (min.)
Class V (5) crushed gravel	6 bags
4x6 x 10' pressure-treated timbers	2
2x6 x 12' (12" o.c. joist spacing)	19
1-1/2" corner angles	22
7" reinforcing angles (or 2x4 x 11" blocks)	25
5/4x6 x 12' decking (Trex Brasilia Cayenne)	25
1x8 x 12' matching skirt board	5
Joist hanger nails	2 lbs.
1-5/8" deck screws	5 lbs.
3" deck screws	2 lbs.
2" stainless steel trim head screws	2 lbs.
Fastenmaster IQ deck fasteners (100 s.f. boxes)	2
1x4 x 10' temporary stretchers (for layout)	2

Cutting list

KEY	QTY.	SIZE & DESCRIPTION
A	2	3-1/2" x 5-1/2" x 120" beams
B	13	1-1/2" x 5-1/2" x 135" joists
C	2	1-1/2" x 5-1/2" x 138" rim joists
D	7	1-1/2" x 5-1/2" x 48" stair stringers
E	24	1" x 5-1/2" x 138" deck boards (cut in place)
F	2	1" x 5-1/2" x 55-1/2" stair treads
G	2	3/4" x 7-1/2" x 140" skirt board
H	2	3/4" x 7-1/2" x 138-1/2" skirt board
J	1	3/4" x 7-1/2" x 48" skirt board
K	1	3/4" x 7-1/2" x 24" skirt board
L	1	3/4" x 7-1/2" x 57-1/2" riser
M	6	1-1/2" x 5-1/2" x 7-1/2" blocking
P	10	1-1/2" x 5-1/2" x 10-1/2" blocking
Q	25	1-1/2" x 3-1/2" x 11" joist supports (can be used instead of metal reinforcing angles)
R	40	1/4" x 5-1/2" spacers

2 Take diagonal measurements and tap one beam forward or back to square the beams. Temporary stretchers hold the beams parallel.

3 Screw on angle brackets at each joist location instead of toenailing, which can split and weaken the joists and knock the beam out of square.

4 Install the middle and end joists, then screw on the rim joists, using clamps (or a helper) to hold them in place.

the joists straight and to hold the outside joists up (Photo 4). The decking will hold the outside joists up when the rim joist is removed later.

Set the other joists on the beams and fasten them to the beams and rim joists. Reinforce the outside corners with additional blocking (Photo 5). Finally, mark the center of the joists and run blocking between each pair of joists. Set the blocking 1/2 in. to the side of the center mark, alternating from side to side, so that the blocking doesn't end up in the gap between the deck boards.

Add a step

The deck surface should be no more than 8 in. above the ground where you step up on it. If it's close, just build up the ground or

add concrete pavers. Otherwise, add a step.

To cantilever the stairs, extend the stair stringers underneath four deck joists, then join the floor joists and stair stringers with reinforcing angles (as we did) or wood 2x4s, which are less expensive (Photo 6). Use a screw first to hold the angles or 2x4 blocks in place, then finish fastening them with nails, which have greater shear strength.

The 5/4 (nominal) decking shown called for a maximum spacing between stair stringers of 9 in. on center, but you can space stringers 16 in. on center if you use solid wood.

Hidden fasteners create a clean look

The deck boards shown were attached with hidden fasteners (see Materials List). Other types of hidden fasteners are available—or

5 For strong connections at the corners, set corner blocking between the last two joists, then nail the rim joist from both directions.

FASTEN FROM BOTH SIDES

6 Frame the steps next. You can avoid additional footings by hanging stringers from the deck joists with metal angles or 2x4s.

STRINGER

7 Attach the deck boards. Decks look best when you use hidden fasteners, but they make installation slower. Trim the deck boards flush with the rim joist when you're done.

HIDDEN FASTENER

RIM JOIST

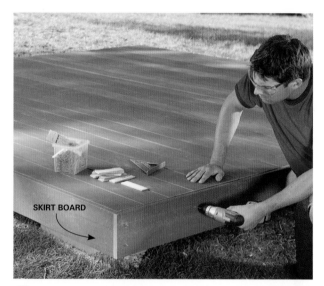

8 Wrap the deck with skirt boards that match the decking, driving trim head screws just below the surface at the spacer locations (see Figure A).

SKIRT BOARD

you can use deck screws, which create lots of holes but save time and money.

Start with a full board at one side, aligning it with the edge of the rim joist. Leave the boards long at both ends, then cut them back later all at once so the edges are straight. Use four 1/4-in. spacers between each pair of boards as you fasten them, but check the distance to the rim joist after every four boards and adjust spacing if necessary so you won't have to rip your last board.

At the next to the last board, remove the rim joist and mark and cut the ends off the joists so the last deck board lines up with the edge of the rim joist. Reinstall the rim joist and attach the last boards.

Nail 1/4-in. spacers ripped from treated wood to the rim joist every 16 in. so water won't get trapped against the rim joist. Screw on skirt boards with two screws at each spacer (Photo 8). Attach the decking to the steps after the skirt boards are fastened. Finally, finish the steps (Photo 9).

RISER

SPACER

NOTCH HERE

SKIRT BOARD

9 Screw skirt boards to the sides of the steps for a finished look, then measure, cut and attach a riser board to the face of the steps.

Quick & easy paths
Paths you can build in a weekend
without breaking the bank or your back

Most books and articles on paths show you how to build paths the hard way, by digging out tons of soil and bringing in tons of gravel to create a sturdy path that will last almost forever. And this backbreaking, costly method is definitely the best way to build a front walkway or other primary path.

But there are easier alternatives. If you want a more casual path and don't mind if it needs occasional upkeep or eventually becomes a bit uneven, consider these labor- and money-saving approaches. We'll cover the pros and cons of mulch and gravel, stepping-stone and planted paths and give you some building tips for each.

Mulch and gravel paths

Mulch and gravel are the cheapest path materials you can buy, and they make construction simple too. All you have to do is remove the sod, roll out landscape fabric and spread the mulch or gravel.

Mulch and gravel paths can be meandering, wood chip–covered trails or carefully planned designs, and range from casual to formal depending on the design and edging material. You can choose from a wide variety of loose materials including coarse bark, decorative mulch, washed stones and crushed gravel or shells.

Mulch

Bark, wood chips and other types of organic mulch make soft paths that blend well with natural settings. Since these path materials are lighter than stone, they're easier to haul and spread. Mulch is also a bit cheaper than gravel or stone pebbles. Remember, though, that organic paths decompose over time, so you'll have to rejuvenate them every two to five years with new material. Also, don't use bark, wood chips or mulch for paths that run through areas with poor drainage or that are wet. It'll lead to a soggy path.

You'll find bags of mulch at home centers, but for the best selection of organic materials for a path, check your local nursery or landscape supplier. Depending on how big your path is, it may be cheaper to have bulk material delivered than to buy bags. Call the public works department at your city hall or check with local tree trimming services. They often have piles of wood chips or mulch that are free for the hauling.

Gravel

For a path that's more formal or longer lasting than a mulch path, consider washed gravel, crushed stone or crushed shells. These materials last indefinitely and only need occasional weeding to look their best. If you want to run a wheelbarrow or lawn mower along the path, choose crushed stone rather than smooth pebbles. The jagged edges of crushed stone lock together to form a firm surface. Crushed stone is also less likely to get kicked out into the yard.

Gravel for paths is sold by type and size. Smaller stones, averaging under 1/2 in., are best for paths because they offer more comfort underfoot and pack together better. Visit your local nursery or landscape supply specialist to see what's available in your area. Gravel is usually sold by the ton. Measure the length and width of the path. Take these measurements

METAL EDGING

BRICK

to the supplier and ask for help figuring out the quantity of gravel you need. Unless your path is very short, it usually makes sense to have the material delivered. Gravel for a path 3 in. deep and 3 ft. wide will cost about $1.50 per linear foot.

Gravel paths do have a few limitations, though. The stones can get tracked into the house, so don't use them near entries. And gravel paths are a bad choice in areas where you have to shovel snow off them. The gravel can end up in your lawn or flower beds.

Borders and edging

Gravel or mulch paths require edging to keep the material from spreading out onto your lawn or flower bed. You can also add a border or an edge as a design element. Here are some common types of edging you can use:

■ Plastic landscape edging is cheap. And it's fast and easy to install. If you object to the look of the rounded top edge, hide it with a border of plants.

■ Steel or aluminum edging forms a crisp edge that gives the path a neat appearance. It costs more than plastic, though, and is less forgiving on sloped terrain.

■ Brick and stone borders are attractive and versatile, but they're more expensive and a lot more work to install.

■ Concrete edging is less expensive than brick or stone but has the same advantages. Newer

WOOD CHIPS

COCOA BEAN

CYPRESS BARK

CRUSHED
LIMESTONE

CRUSHED,
WASHED
GRAVEL

PEA ROCK

types that look like random pieces of tumbled stone are a great lower-cost alternative to a real stone border.

■ Landscape timbers are an economical alternative to stone or brick borders. They're especially useful for building shallow steps on gradually sloping terrain.

Tips for building mulch and gravel paths

■ Rent a gas-powered sod cutter to remove grass if the path is long. For short paths, use a garden spade to slice off the sod.

■ Set edging so it ends up about an inch above the fill material.

■ Use a spacer stick cut to the width of the path as a guide when you set the edging or border. You won't have to keep pulling out the tape measure to make sure the edges run parallel.

■ Cover the soil with landscape fabric to deter weeds and prevent the fill material from mixing with the soil. Don't use plastic. It'll catch water and create a soggy path.

■ Have gravel delivered, especially if you need more than a half ton.

■ If you want a path that's firm enough to roll a wheelbarrow on, use crushed stone and tamp it after leveling it. (Pea rock or other rounded stone won't compact.) Use a hand tamper for short paths. Rent a vibrating-plate tamper for long paths.

Planted paths

Including ground cover plants in your path makes a stone walkway easier in two ways: First, you can skip the thick, compacted gravel base underneath. That eliminates the backbreaking digging, plus the hauling and compacting of gravel. Without the solid base, the stones will shift and become uneven, but the plants will hide that. The second advantage is that you don't have to spend extra time laying the stones perfectly. The plants will hide wide gaps.

familyhandyman.com
For a unique, old-world look, build a path from brick and stone. Go to familyhandyman.com and search brick stone pathway.

There are quite a few perennial plants that can withstand foot traffic and will grow between stones. Check with your local nursery to see what's available that will grow in your area. Here are some ground cover plants that can tolerate some foot traffic: Creeping Thyme, Blue Star Creeper, Brass Buttons, Creeping Mazus and Sedum.

Tips for building a planted path

■ Arrange the stones along the walkway, leaving at least 4 in. between them for plants. Then cut along the edge of the stones with a flat spade to outline the path.

■ Slice off a layer of sod and soil about 1-1/2 in. deep.

■ Spread a 1/2-in. layer of sand. This will allow the stones to settle in slightly and keep them from rocking.

■ Choose plants that will stand up to traffic and grow in the available light and soil type.

■ Water the new plants frequently for the first few months until the plants are well established.

■ Pull weeds and grass from between the stones every few weeks to prevent them from overrunning the plants.

Stepping-stone paths

Tips for building a stepping-stone path

- Arrange stones so the distance from the center of one to the center of the next one is 20 to 24 in.
- Set the stones in place and cut around them with a spade or drywall keyhole saw. Then lift the stone and dig out the grass and a little soil.
- Spread a 1/2- to 1-in.-thick layer of sand under the stone if you want to make leveling the stones easier. Sand is easier to work with than soil. A 60-lb. bag of sand is enough for about four to six stones.
- Set the top of the stepping-stones about 1 in. above the soil level. This will give you a dry place to step while still allowing you to run a lawn mower over the path.

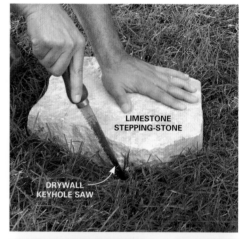

LIMESTONE STEPPING-STONE

DRYWALL KEYHOLE SAW

TROWEL

S tepping-stones are the fastest, easiest way to build a path. There's very little digging involved. And although the stone is heavy, a little goes a long way. Since there's distance between the stones, you don't have to worry about leveling them with one another. Stepping-stone paths also cost less because you'll cover more distance with less stone. Stones that are flat and about 18 in. across and 2 in. thick are ideal. Check your local landscape supplier or quarry to see what's available. If you're building a short stepping-stone path, you can usually pick the stones you want from the pallet or pile of stones on hand at the supplier. For longer paths, ask for help figuring the quantity and have the stone delivered. If you're lucky enough to live in an area with naturally occurring outcroppings of stone, you may find stepping-stones free for the hauling.

You can also make attractive stepping-stone paths using 12-in. square or round concrete patio blocks. These are available in a wide selection of colors and textures from home centers, landscape suppliers and masonry dealers. Search online for "patio blocks" to see the variety.

Path in a wheelbarrow

This garden path is as easy to build as it is to look at and walk on. A bundle or two of cedar shakes, a roll of landscape fabric, a few bags of mulch and a couple of hours are all it takes to build it.

To create the path edging, cut 18-in.-long cedar shakes in half, then pound the 9-in. sections about halfway into the ground. Shakes are naturally rot-resistant and should last 5 to 10 years or more. And since they're tapered, they're easy to install. Bear in mind that shakes will split and break if you try to pound them into soil with lots of rocks, roots or heavy clay; this path works best in a garden setting with loose soil.

The landscape fabric helps prevent weeds from growing in the path, and creates a barrier so the dirt below remains separate from the path materials above.

The path material can be wood chips, shredded bark, decorative stone—just about anything.

Here's how to do it in three steps:

WEAR YOUR SAFETY GLASSES

CEDAR SHAKES

1 Pound the cedar shakes into the soil using a small mallet. Stagger every other shake, overlapping the previous shake by about 1/2 in.

tip If you're breaking shakes as you drive them in, place a scrap 2x6 on top of each shake and pound on that. The 2x6 helps distribute the blow more evenly across the top of the shake.

2 Trim or fold the fabric so it follows the contour of the cedar shake edging. On sloped ground, use U-shaped sod staples to hold the fabric.

MULCH

3 Install a 2- to 3-in. layer of wood chips, shredded bark or stone over the landscape fabric.

Simple window planter

You can put together this simple window planter in less than an hour. For each planter, you'll need three 6-in. clay pots, 3 ft. each of 1x10 and 1x3, and 2 ft. of 2x8.

Cut the 1x10 and 1x3 to length (see photos for dimensions). Pot diameters vary, so size the holes by scribing and cutting out a 6-in. circle from cardboard to ensure that the pot will rest on its rim (Photo 1). Keep testing until you find the size. Then lay out and cut the openings.

Use a 5-gallon pail lid to scribe the bracket curves (Photo 2). Make sure the grain runs parallel to the shelf for strength. Smooth off the rough edges and paint the parts before assembly—especially if you want the two-tone look. Then screw the parts together with 2-in. exterior screws.

Mount the shelf to the wall by screwing through the hanging strip into the wall framing.

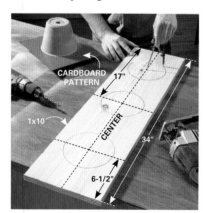

1 Mark the 6-in.-diameter holes with a compass. Then drill 1/2-in. starter holes and cut out the openings with a jigsaw.

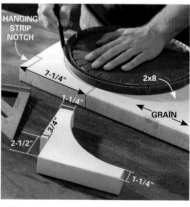

2 Mark the notch for the hanging strip and both 1-1/4-in. ends on the brackets. Draw the curve and cut the openings with a jigsaw.

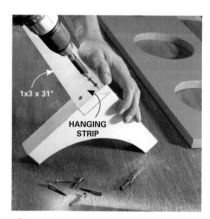

3 Predrill and screw the hanging strip to the brackets. Then center and screw the shelf to the brackets and to the hanging strip.

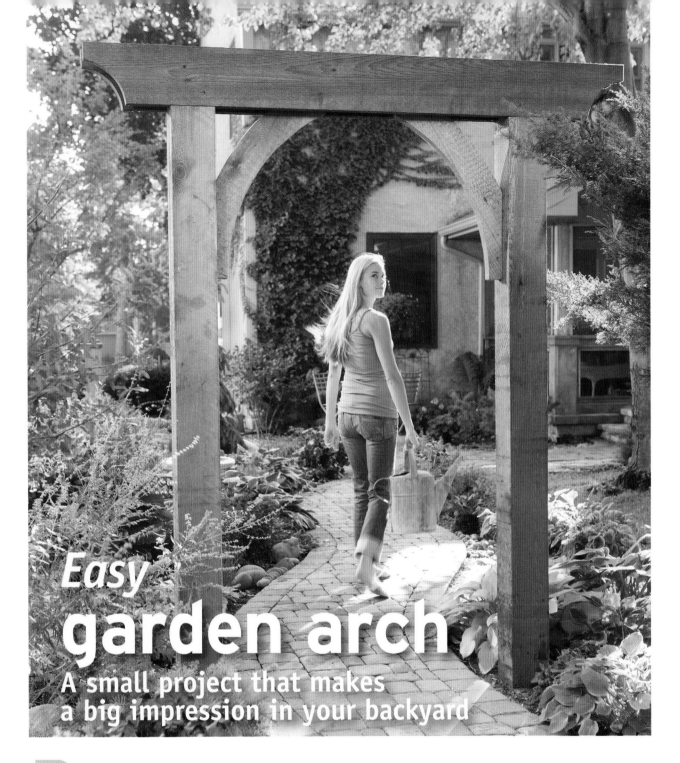

Easy
garden arch
A small project that makes a big impression in your backyard

Building an arch is one of the easiest ways to give your landscape a striking centerpiece. And this arch is easier than most. Made from just six parts, it can be built in less than a day—even if you're a rookie carpenter. The design is versatile, too: The arch can become a gateway in a fence, frame a walkway through a hedge or stand alone in your yard or garden. You can stain it for a rustic look or paint it for a more formal look.

Materials

The arch shown here is made from cedar. Built from pressure-treated lumber, it would cost about half as much.

Depending on where you live, you may have other choices of rot-resistant lumber available, such as cypress or redwood. If you choose treated lumber, you'll find everything you need for this project at home centers. If you choose another wood species, you may have to special-order lumber or visit a traditional lumberyard.

You'll need only standard tools like a drill, a circular saw and a jigsaw. Make sure your framing square is a standard model (16 x 24 in., with a longer leg that's 2 in. wide). If yours is an oddball, buy a standard version so you can easily mark out the brackets (see Photo 2). A few days before you dig the postholes, call 811 to have underground utility lines marked.

Cut the parts

To get started, cut notches in the tops of the posts (Photo 1). If you're using "rough-sawn" lumber as we did, you may have to change the length and depth of these notches to suit your 2x8 headers. (The dimensions of rough-sawn lumber vary.) Set the cutting depth of your circular saw to 1-1/2 in. to make the crosscuts for the notches. Then set your saw to full depth to make the other cuts.

Next cut the 2x8 headers to length and mark arcs at the ends as shown in Figure A. To mark the curves, use the bottom of a 5-gallon bucket or any circle that's 10 to 11 in. in diameter. Cut the curves with a jigsaw.

The curved brackets may look complicated, but they're easy to mark since they're based on a standard framing square. After marking with the square (Photo 2), set a nail in your sawhorse 20 in. from the edge of the board. Carefully adjust the position of the board until both corner marks of the bracket are 24 in. from the nail. Then, holding your pencil at the 24-in. mark on the tape, draw an arc. To draw the second arc, move your pencil to the 29-in. mark on the tape (Photo 3). Cut the straight edges of the brackets with a circular saw and the arcs with a jigsaw. If the curves turn out a bit wavy, smooth them with an orbital or belt sander. Don't be too fussy, though. Nobody will notice small imperfections.

Put it all together

Mark one header 12 in. from both ends and lay out the posts, aligned with the marks. Take measurements at the other end to make sure the posts are perfectly parallel. Drive 3-1/2-in. screws through the posts and into the header. At the tops of the brackets, drive 3-in. screws at a slight angle so they won't poke through the face of the header (Photo 4). Set 1-1/2-in.-thick blocks under the other ends of the brackets. Then drive screws at an angle through the sides of the brackets and into the posts. Be sure to drill 1/8-in. pilot holes so you don't split the brackets. Set the second header in place and screw it to the posts. Note: The brackets are not centered on the posts, so there's a 1-in. gap between the second header and the brackets.

Set it up

You'll set the arch posts into 10-in.-diameter holes 30 in. deep. But before you move the arch into place, screw on a temporary 2x4 "stretcher" 30 in. from the post bottoms. Then round up a helper or two and set the posts into the holes. Patiently level and plumb the arch, using stakes and 2x4s to brace it (Photo 5). Be careful not to nudge the posts out of position as you fill the holes with concrete. Let the concrete harden for at least four hours before you finish the wood. Brush on two coats of clear penetrating wood finish to deepen the color of the wood and repel moisture.

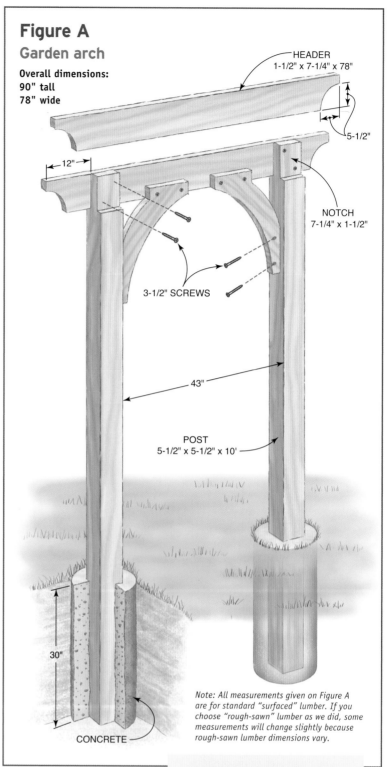

Figure A
Garden arch

Overall dimensions:
90" tall
78" wide

HEADER
1-1/2" x 7-1/4" x 78"

5-1/2"

12"

NOTCH
7-1/4" x 1-1/2"

3-1/2" SCREWS

43"

POST
5-1/2" x 5-1/2" x 10'

30"

CONCRETE

Note: All measurements given on Figure A are for standard "surfaced" lumber. If you choose "rough-sawn" lumber as we did, some measurements will change slightly because rough-sawn lumber dimensions vary.

Materials list

ITEM	QTY.
6x6 x 10' (posts)	2
2x8 x 8' (headers)	2
2x10 x 8' (brackets)	1
2x4 x 8' (stretcher, stakes, braces)	3
Concrete mix (60-lb. bags)	3
3" and 3-1/2" screws	

1 Notch the tops of the posts. Cut as deep as you can from both sides with a circular saw, then finish the cuts with a handsaw.

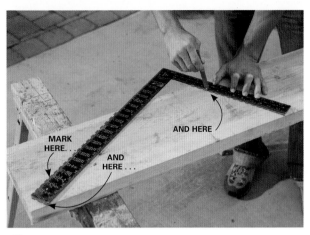

MARK HERE...
AND HERE...
AND HERE

2 Mark the brackets without fussy measurements or geometry—just align a framing square with the edges of a 2x10 and make three marks.

3 Draw perfect curves fast using a tape measure to guide your pencil. Cut out the bracket and use it as a pattern for the other bracket.

BRACKET
HEADER

4 Screw through the posts and brackets into the header. That way, one header will have no visible screws. Screw through the second header into the posts.

STRETCHER
SHIMS

5 Set the arch level and plumb before you pour concrete into the postholes. Wedge shims under the stretcher until the header is level, then plumb and brace the posts.

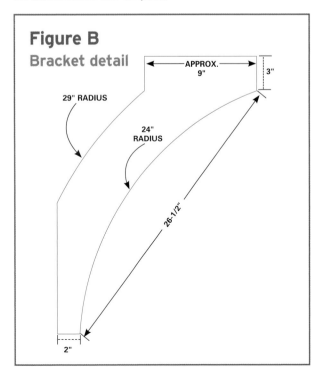

Figure B
Bracket detail

APPROX. 9"
3"
29" RADIUS
24" RADIUS
26-1/2"
2"

Pint-sized water gardens
Mini ponds perfect for patios or decks

Container gardens with aquatic plants create more mystery than plants potted in soil. Plus, they're extremely low maintenance. Top them off with water before you go on vacation, and they're still beautiful when you come home. Container water gardens are inexpensive and easy to build, too. So here's how to get into the swim of things with a container water garden.

What you need

For a basic garden, you need at least an 18- to 20-in. plastic container that's 7 to 8 in. deep, a small submersible pump, a spouting ornament, plants, clear vinyl tubing, clean cat litter, pea gravel or small pebbles and a nylon stocking. Most items are readily available at larger garden centers or online (see "Supplies," p. 62).

How to build it

The photos show you how. Here are a few additional tips:

■ The floor is two tiered to allow for different types of plants; the lilies planted on the deep side have stems that float upward and extend horizontally, while the "marginal" plants—those that grow upright and favor shallower water—stand on the higher side. The partition that separates the two sides can be made from stone, bricks or other heavy material.

■ Pea gravel both beautifies your water garden and acts as a lid over the unpotted soil so it can't circulate and darken the water. Rinse the pea gravel before adding it to the container.

■ For extra protection, place the pump in a nylon stocking before putting it in the cup, then stuff the extra nylon over the pump. This filtering is crucial; otherwise, pebbles and cat litter will be drawn into the pump and clog it. A well-filtered pump will run for months; a clogged pump must be dug up, which fouls the water.

■ Small submersible pumps have adjustable pressure, so before burying the pump, place it in a bucket of water, plug it in and adjust the pressure of the jet of water coming out of the spouter.

■ Fill a couple of buckets with tap water, then let them sit for a day or two to allow chlorine to evaporate and water temperature to moderate. Pour the water in gradually—it should be as clear as a mountain stream.

■ Aquatic plants thrive on direct sunlight, so a bright sunny spot is ideal. If possible, position the container near an electrical outlet for the pump.

Wind can wreak havoc with tall plants by pushing the containers off their pedestals. Finding a wind-free space helps solve this problem and ensures the fountain arc from the spouting ornament looks and sounds the way you want it to.

Care and maintenance

Taking care of water gardens is a breeze. Top them off as water evaporates and scoop off the occasional dead leaf or bit of algae.

Plants maintain water clarity by absorbing decaying matter through their roots as food. But if

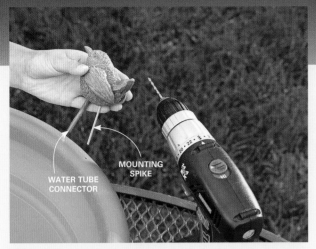

1 Drill a small hole in the rim of the container to mount the spouting ornament. If you need to bend the support spike to level or position the spouter, grip it with two pairs of pliers so you don't crack the ornament.

WATER TUBE CONNECTOR

MOUNTING SPIKE

2 Spread the soil of the lily or other deep-water plants in one half of the container, then add cat litter to create a level floor.

PEA GRAVEL

CAT LITTER

3 Add a partition to divide the container into halves. Plant the shallow-growing marginal plants and spread more cat litter over the soil. On the low side, nestle a plastic cup for the pump in the cat litter, keeping the pump covered with plastic to prevent gravel from falling in.

PLASTIC COVER

MARGINAL PLANTS

FLAGSTONE PARTITION

4 Spread pea gravel over the cat litter. Keep the floor on the lily side lower to allow the lily stems room to extend upward when you add water.

LOWER SIDE

PEA GRAVEL

the water starts looking gunky, remove the plants, rinse the container and refill.

For any plants needing a boost, press a fertilizer pellet into the potting soil. You can also add a Mosquito Dunk a couple times in the summer to kill mosquito larvae without posing harm to people or pets. Smaller containers will only need a small piece.

You can overwinter hardy water lilies by wrapping them in a damp towel and storing them in a cool basement or garage corner. Other plants are

MOSQUITO DUNK

FERTILIZER PELLETS

5 Connect the pump to the spouter with vinyl tubing. Use a transition piece of 1/2-in. tubing if necessary to connect the 3/8-in. tube to the pump. Press the pump into the cup so that the suction cups anchor it to the bottom.

3/8" TUBING

SECTION OF 1/2" TUBING

SUCTION CUPS

relatively inexpensive and grow rapidly, so in cold climates, buy them anew each year and treat as annuals.

For a small container, plant a dwarf lily so the pads don't completely cover the surface of the water as they grow. For larger water gardens, you can add a floating plant like water hyacinth, duckweed or water lettuce.

A dish-style garden is too small for koi or goldfish, but larger containers, like whiskey barrels or larger terra-cotta pots, are ideal. (Note: Water in metal containers usually gets too warm for fish.) Fish help keep the garden clean by eating algae, decaying plant material and mosquito larvae.

Supplies

Water pumps. planetrena.com

Spouting wren ornament. marylandaquatic.com

NYLON FILTER

6 Cover the pump with a nylon stocking filter to keep gravel from clogging the pump, and then cover the pump with pea gravel.

One-hour water garden

If you want an instant water garden, simply slip a plastic barrel liner into a decorative wooden barrel, set some pavers of various heights in place to act as pedestals, and then perch a few potted aquatic plants on top. Just make sure to position the plants at the depth indicated on the plant tag or information sheet. The only drawback to this approach is that the container won't look as natural close up— you can see the plastic pots below the surface. You can even add a spouter to the barrel; the pump can simply sit on a pedestal without a cup.

If you can't find a plastic barrel liner, you can make a watertight terra-cotta container by plugging the drain hole with plumber's epoxy and applying two coats of polyurethane.

LINER

PAVER PEDESTALS

POLYURETHANE

PLUMBER'S EPOXY

Backyard
spring
Build this bubbling fountain in 4 hours

If you've ever been to Yellowstone, you probably remember the magic of the natural springs. In less than half a day, you can build a small spring for you to enjoy at home. Here's what you need:

■ A large sturdy tub or bucket (about a 15-gallon size).

■ A piece of pond liner large enough to line the bucket plus an additional foot on each side. The liner shown here is 5 ft. square.

■ A small fountain pump (this one moved 210 gallons per hour).

■ A piece of flexible braided plastic tubing the diameter of the pump outlet and cut to the length of the bucket height.

■ A hose clamp to connect the tubing to the pump.

■ A brick to rest the pump on.

■ A square piece of heavy-gauge, galvanized hardware cloth with a 1/4-in. grid, cut 6 to 8 in. larger than the diameter of the bucket.

■ About 40 lbs. of round rocks 1-1/2 to 3 in. in diameter. Mexican beach pebbles from a local nursery were used here.

You can tuck this spring fountain in the corner of a patio where you can easily see and hear the water. It can go anywhere in your yard or garden, but you'll need an outdoor outlet nearby.

Dig it in

■ Dig a hole the size of your bucket, but slightly deeper. Place the top lip of the bucket 2-1/2 in. below the surface of the patio or ground.

■ Place the bucket in the hole and backfill around it.

■ Line the inside of the bucket with your pond liner. Extend the liner out at least 8 in. beyond the diameter of the bucket, more if you want your spring to shoot up higher. You want the liner to catch any water splashing on the rocks and direct the runoff back into the bucket. Curl up the edge of the liner to create a ledge for that purpose. Create a ledge by wedging the liner between two bricks.

■ Place the brick and the pump in the center of the bucket. Connect the tubing to the pump outlet with a hose clamp.

■ Follow the manufacturer's instructions for running the cord. Don't bury it. **Caution:** Plug the cord into a GFCI-protected outlet.

■ Place the hardware cloth over the bucket and snip a small hole

in the center to allow the tubing through. The hardware cloth should be larger than the diameter of the bucket.

■ Place the stones and brick on top of the hardware cloth and fill the bucket with water.

■ Turn the pump on and adjust the tubing, wedging it between the rocks to get the desired effect. You can restrict the flow of the water by pinching the pipe with wire or buying a flow restrictor from your pump supplier. The diameter of the pipe will determine how high the water bubbles up.

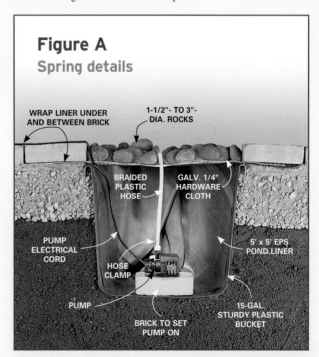

Figure A
Spring details

WRAP LINER UNDER AND BETWEEN BRICK

1-1/2"- TO 3"- DIA. ROCKS

BRAIDED PLASTIC HOSE

GALV. 1/4" HARDWARE CLOTH

PUMP ELECTRICAL CORD

5' x 5' EPS POND LINER

HOSE CLAMP

PUMP

15-GAL. STURDY PLASTIC BUCKET

BRICK TO SET PUMP ON

Soothing fountain

Inexpensive, simple to build and a great place for the neighborhood birds to freshen up

This quaint fountain is proof that good things come in small packages and you can build it in an afternoon. It's a "disappearing fountain" so there's no exposed standing water. This means there's less maintenance since there's less chance debris and critters will wind up in the water. Yet it provides the soothing sight and sound of running water people love. Another bonus—since birds love moving water, there's a chance you'll attract some of these outdoor friends.

You can personalize your fountain in a number of ways:

■ Surround it with any type of rock. Shown is a natural wall stone, but you can use modular concrete retaining-wall blocks, boulders or flagstone.

■ Top it off with any type of small stone. Shown is a decorative rock called "Western Sunset." You can use pebbles, lava stone or special rocks you've collected in your travels.

■ Use any bowl, dish or plate you want for the water to splash into. The fountain shown incorporates three pieces so the water cascades from one piece into the next.

Let's get started

The fountain shown here utilizes a whiskey barrel liner from a home center for the catch basin, but any large plastic container will do (see Photo 1 on p. 66). Some garden centers sell special pond liners just for this purpose.

Regardless of your soil conditions, nestle your catch basin or

Multiple spray patterns

All four of these interchangeable fountainheads, which provide different looks, came in one package. It only took part of an afternoon to build this fountain, and it didn't take any fancy tools.

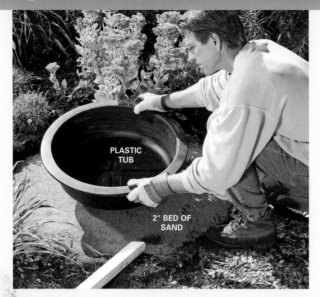

1 Select a location where you'll enjoy your fountain, hollow out a 2-in.-deep area, then level in a bed of sand large enough to accommodate the plastic tub and the rock or block that will surround it.

2 Locate a sturdy plastic flower pot the same height as your plastic tub, cut a hole in the side near the bottom and feed the cord for the electric pump through it. Position this pot right side up in the center of your tub.

3 Cut a hole in the wire hardware cloth (available at home centers) large enough for the pump to fit through, then position the cloth over the tub and bend the edges over the tub lip.

4 Surround the tub with flagstone or concrete retaining-wall blocks to match the rest of your landscape. The upper course should be about 2 in. higher than the top of the tub to help contain the decorative rocks.

liner into a bed of sand. This helps protect the bottom of the tub from sharp rocks and makes it easier to level the tub and the first course of rock.

Construct your fountain so you can gain access to the pump by removing a handful of rocks along with the hardware cloth trap door (Photo 5). This allows you to easily remove the pump for maintenance and for storing it indoors over the winter.

Use a bag of sand as a workbench when drilling the holes in your bowls and dishes (Photo 6). It'll provide a cushion and help prevent breakage.

Many large garden centers and home centers sell water garden pumps and accessories. Or check out:

- lagunaponds.com.
- lg-outdoor.com.
- macarthurwatergardens.com.

Operating tips

Keep your fountain liner full of water and check the level every day or so, especially in hot weather. You can use any thin stick as a dipstick to check the water level. If you run your fountain

5 Cut a small piece of hardware cloth a few inches larger than the access hole to create a removable trap door, then cut a small opening for the pump stem. Cover the top of the hardware cloth with decorative stone.

SMALL OPENING FOR PUMP STEM

REMOVABLE TRAP DOOR

6 Drill a hole in your fountain dish by first scoring the glaze in the center of the bowl with a light tap of a nail (very light!), then boring a hole using a ceramic tile bit. If you need to enlarge the hole, use a larger bit or small file.

CERAMIC TILE BIT

BAG OF SAND

7 Install the fountainhead of your choice. Most pumps can accommodate a range of heads including mushroom-shaped, cup-shaped and fan-shaped patterns (see p. 65). Then fill the tub, plug in the pump and relax.

OTHER FOUNTAIN HEADS

Figure A
How it all goes together

FOUNTAINHEAD

TO GCFI-PROTECTED OUTLET

PUMP ACCESS TRAP DOOR

DECORATIVE ROCK

HARDWARE CLOTH

EXTENSION TUBE

PUMP

1" TO 2" OF SAND

RIGID PLASTIC FLOWER POT

frequently and it splashes water outside the tub, you may need to refill it daily.

Plug your pump into a GFCI-protected outlet—ideally one located next to the fountain. If you use an extension cord, leave it exposed so you know where it is, and be careful working near it with sharp garden tools and mowers.

As a precaution, unplug the fountain when you're not around to watch it (or put it on a timer). If the pump runs dry, it'll burn out.

Most pumps will accept a variety of fountainheads. Bear in mind that with some spray patterns, all the water may not drain back into the tub. You'll have to refill your tub much more often with this type of fountain.

tip Have a little fun selecting your fountain dishes. It's the perfect opportunity to use those I-never-use-'em-but-I-can't-bear-to-throw-'em-out bowls, plates and even teapots.

Gutter deck planter

This lightweight, durable and attractive deck planter is made from a vinyl gutter (10-ft. length), two fascia support brackets and two end caps. It's a snap to make. Glue one of the end caps in place and drill holes in the bottom of the gutter so the water can drain (Photo 1). Slide two fascia support brackets onto the gutter (Photo 2) and glue the other end cap into place. If you want a longer planter, be sure to add extra brackets spaced about every 2 ft.—dirt is heavy.

To prevent the soil from slipping through the drainage holes, line the gutter with newspaper or put shards of old broken clay pots along the bottom.

Shallow planters like these have a tendency to dry out. To cut watering time in half, mix water-absorbing polymer gel crystals (available at garden centers) with your potting mix. Or buy bags of soilless potting mix with the polymer crystals already added.

If you want a color other than white, use a spray paint formulated for plastic. Screw the planter to your deck rail (Photo 3), fill it with potting mix and add your plants. Enjoy!

1 Cut a 2-ft. length of vinyl gutter and glue one of the end caps into place with kitchen and bath adhesive caulk. Drill 1/2-in. drainage holes every 4 in. along the bottom of the gutter.

2 Slide both fascia support brackets onto the gutter and glue the other end cap into place.

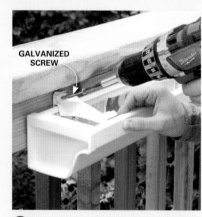

3 Screw the planter to the deck rail through the fascia support brackets using galvanized screws.

3/8" REBAR

1/2" IRON PIPE

HOOP

WIRE LOOP

BENT UPRIGHT

16-GAUGE WIRE

HACKSAW

Rebar plant cage

Covered with vines, this rustic metal plant cage makes an attractive addition to your flower garden. In the vegetable patch, it's a great support for peppers or tomatoes. It's built from inexpensive concrete reinforcing steel (rebar) connected by twisted wire.

You'll need three 10-ft. lengths of 3/8-in. (No. 3) rebar (you'll have a little extra) and about 20 ft. of 16- or 18-gauge wire. You'll find 3/8-in. rebar at home centers. Ask the supplier to cut standard 20-ft. lengths in half to make it easier to haul.

1 Bend 10-ft. lengths of 3/8-in. rebar around a 5-gallon bucket to form two arches as shown. Drill two holes in the side of the bucket and loop a wire through the holes and around the rebar to hold it in place while you do the bending. Slip a 3-ft. length of 1/2-in. pipe over the rebar for better leverage and control. Use the same technique for bending the hoops, but wrap the rebar completely around the bucket to form a circle. Then cut the straight section off with a hacksaw, leaving the hoop and a few inches of overlap. Wrap and twist-tie wire around the overlap to form the two hoops.

2 Stack the two hoops on the ground. Poke the ends of the two arches a few inches into the ground inside the hoops. Twist a 12-in. length of wire around the intersection of the two arches to secure them. Cut off the extra wire. Then slide the first loop up to about 16 in. from the top and wire it in place. Stand back and eyeball the hoop to make sure it's level and the uprights are evenly spaced before you tighten the tie wires. Repeat this process for the second hoop, leaving about 16 in. between hoops.

HOOPS CONNECTED

TWISTED WIRE

Gurgling fountain

As simple as they come

You can enjoy the soothing sounds of a fountain in your backyard without going through the time and expense of building a water garden. This simple wall fountain will take less than a day to assemble.

Fill the cracks inside an old whiskey barrel with clear silicone caulk to make it watertight. Mount the wall fountain on an ivy-covered trellis that's sturdy enough to support the fountain. The trellis and ivy cover up the 1/2-in.-diameter plastic tube that runs from the pump in the barrel below to the "mouth" of the fountain. The vines also mask the electrical cord running from the pump to a nearby outdoor outlet. Caution: Plug the cord into a GFCI-protected outlet. Hide the pump in the barrel behind rocks and such aquatic plants as umbrella palm, water poppy, chameleon plant and variegated sweet flag. These are all shade tolerant; if you have full sun, you can grow water lilies too.

Materials

- A small pump capable of circulating 140 gallons of water an hour
- A half whiskey barrel
- 1/2-in. plastic tubing (hardware store)

Find these materials at a well-stocked garden shop or nursery or lilypons.com. Improvise the wall fountain from a mask made of terra cotta, stone, concrete or plastic or from other interesting wall-hung objects found at antique stores, nurseries or garden centers.

4

Garage improvements

If a tidy, functional garage is on your wish list, you'll find some great ways to get started right here. In one morning, you can organize all of your stuff with the wall system shown on p. 72. Then you can build a sturdy workbench where you can make projects for all around the house. Noisy garage door? You can fix it fast and save the cost of a service call. Plus, find lots of clever accessories for the garage, including two styles of garage door opening screens that you can install to turn your garage into a screen room!

Organize your garage in
one morning

There are lots of ways to create more storage space in your garage, but you won't find another system that's as simple, inexpensive or versatile as this one. It begins with a layer of plywood fastened over drywall or bare studs. Then you just screw on a variety of hooks, hangers, shelves and baskets to suit your needs. That's it. The plywood base lets you quickly mount any kind of storage hardware in any spot—no searching for studs. And because you can place hardware wherever you want (not only at studs), you can arrange items close together to make the most of your wall space. As your needs change, you'll appreciate the versatility of this storage wall too; just unscrew shelves or hooks to rearrange the whole system.

Shown here are three types of storage supplies: wire shelves, wire baskets, and a variety of hooks, hangers and brackets (see p. 73). Selecting and arranging these items to suit your stuff can be the most time-consuming part of this project. To simplify that task, outline the dimensions of your plywood wall on the garage floor with masking tape. Then gather all the stuff you want to store and lay it out on your outline. Arrange and rearrange items to make the most of your wall space. Then make a list of the hardware you need before you head off to the hardware store or home center.

Materials and planning

The section of wall shown here is 6 x 16 ft. Everything you need is available at home centers. Shown is 3/4-in.-thick "BC" grade plywood, which has one side sanded smooth. You could save a few bucks by using 3/4-in. OSB (oriented strand board), also known as chip board, or MDF (medium-density fiberboard). But don't use particleboard; it doesn't hold screws well enough for this job.

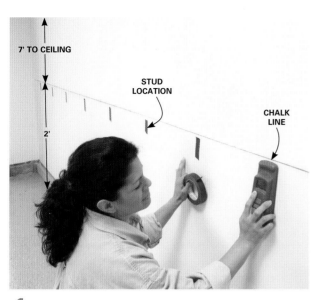

7' TO CEILING

STUD LOCATION

CHALK LINE

2'

1 Snap a level chalk line to mark the bottom edge of the plywood. Locate studs and mark them with masking tape.

2-1/4" SCREW

SUPPORT BLOCK

2 Screw temporary blocks to studs at the chalk line. Start a few screws in the plywood. Rest the plywood on the blocks and screw it to studs.

MIRROR SUPPORT HOOK

Storage supplies for every need

Wire closet shelves are sturdy and inexpensive, and they don't collect dust like solid shelving. They come in lengths up to 12 ft. and you can cut them to any length using a hacksaw or bolt cutters. Standard depths are 12, 16 and 20 in. You'll get more shelving for your money by cutting up long sections than by buying shorter sections. Brackets and support clips (Photo 4) are usually sold separately.

Wire or plastic baskets are perfect for items that won't stay put on shelves (like balls and other toys) and for bags of charcoal or fertilizer that tend to tip and spill. They're also convenient because they're mobile; hang them on hooks and you can lift them off to tote all your tools or toys to the garden or sandbox. You'll find baskets in a variety of shapes and sizes at home centers and discount stores. You can use just about any type of hook to hang baskets. Heavy-duty mirror supports fit these baskets perfectly.

Hooks, hangers and brackets handle all the odd items that don't fit on shelves or in baskets. Basic hooks are often labeled for a specific purpose, but you can use them in other ways. Big "ladder brackets," for example, can hold several long-handled tools. "Ceiling hooks" for bikes also work on walls. Don't write off the wall area below the plywood—it's prime space for items that don't protrude far from the wall. We drove hooks into studs to hang an extension ladder.

3 Set the upper course of plywood in place and screw it to studs. Stagger the vertical joints between the upper and lower courses.

VERTICAL JOINT

12" SCREW SPACING

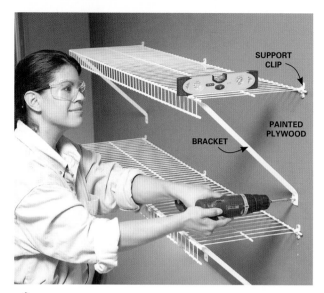

4 Fasten the back edge of shelves with plastic clips. Set a level on the shelf and install the end brackets. Then add center brackets every 2 ft.

SUPPORT CLIP

PAINTED PLYWOOD

BRACKET

Aside from standard hand tools, all you need to complete this project is a drill to drive screws and a circular saw to cut plywood. You may also need a helper when handling plywood—full sheets are awkward and heavy.

This project doesn't require much planning; just decide how much of the wall you want to cover with plywood. You can cover an entire wall floor-to-ceiling or cover any section of a wall. In this garage, the lower 3 ft. of wall and upper 18 in. were left uncovered, since those high and low areas are best used for other types of storage. To make the most of the plywood, a course of full-width sheets was combined with a course of sheets cut in half. If your ceiling height is 9 ft. or less, a single 4-ft.-wide course of plywood may suit your needs.

Cover the wall with plywood

When you've determined the starting height of the plywood, measure up from the floor at one end of the wall and drive a nail. Then measure down to the nail from the ceiling and use that measurement to make a pencil mark at the other end of the wall. (Don't measure up from the floor, since garage floors often slope.) Hook your chalk line on the nail, stretch it to the pencil mark and snap a line (Photo 1).

Cut the first sheet of plywood to length so it ends at the center of a stud. Place the end you cut in the corner. That way the factory-cut edge will form a tight joint with the factory edge of the next sheet. Be sure to place the rough side of the plywood against the wall. Fasten the plywood with 10d finish nails or screws that are at least 2-1/4 in. long (Photo 2). Shown here are trim screws, which have small heads that are easy to cover with a dab of spackling compound. Drive screws or nails every 12 in. into each stud. If you add a second course of plywood above the first as shown (Photo 3), you'll have to cut the plywood to width. You can use a circular saw, but a table saw gives you faster, straighter cuts. Some home centers and lumberyards cut plywood for free

Garden

5 Acrylic photo frames make great label holders. Just slip in your labels and hot-glue the frames to wire baskets. Frames can be bought for a few bucks at office supply and discount stores.

Sports

Beach Lawn Auto

or for a small charge.

With all the plywood in place, go ahead and mount the hardware, or take a few extra steps to dress up the wall first: You can add 3/4-in. cove molding along the lower edge of the plywood for a neater look and to cover up the chalk line and screw holes left by the support blocks. You can also frame the window trim with doorstop molding to hide small gaps between the trim and the plywood. Caulk gaps between the sheets of plywood and fill screw holes. Finally, prime the plywood, lightly sand it with 100-grit sandpaper and paint it.

Handy hooks

When you're out shopping, you might find elaborate hangers designed to hold specific toys and tools. These specialty hooks are nice, but you don't have to spend a lot just to hang a bike or garden tools. With a little ingenuity, you can hang just about anything on simple screw-in hooks that typically cost about a buck. You can place hooks anywhere on your plywood wall. If you don't put them on the plywood, be sure to locate them at studs.

Drill a hole at a 45-degree angle and turn in a screw hook to hang a bicycle by the front wheel.

Hang ladders on hooks below the plywood for easy access.

More projects online

If you're looking for more garage storage projects, visit **familyhandyman. com** and search for "garage storage." Here are just a few of the projects you'll find: A hang-it-all storage wall, nifty rotating shelves and an above-your-head shelf system that holds a ton! So, if you don't see anything that will work for you here, you will find it online.

Quiet a noisy
garage door

If you have a noisy garage door, the fixes are fairly easy and will take less than an hour. Start by tightening all the door and track hardware (Photo 1). But don't overtighten—that can pull the carriage bolt heads right through the door skin or strip the lag screw holes.

Next, check for worn rollers and hinges (Photo 2). Many track rollers have unsealed bearings that self-destruct after years of rolling around in a dirty environment. The wear can be so severe that the rollers actually wobble as the door operates. If your rollers are worn, consider replacing them with nylon rollers with sealed bearings. One source is garage-doors-and-parts.com. Nylon rollers are quieter and don't require periodic oiling. But they are more expensive.

Replace track rollers one at a time (Photo 2). If your door uses torsion springs mounted on the header above the door, do NOT attempt to replace the rollers in the bottom brackets. Those brackets are under constant spring tension and can cause serious injury if you unbolt them. That's a job for a pro.

Worn hinges are less common than worn rollers. But sloppy hinges make a lot of noise and can cause the door to bind and wear out the tongue-and-groove joints at the door sections. Some play at the hinge is normal. But if you see an oblong hole where the tubular hinge pin mates with the hinge bracket, replace the hinge. Gray dust and metal filings around the hinge pin are early signs of wear.

Once you've replaced the worn door components, spray the hinges, roller bearings (unsealed style), and springs with garage door lube (such as Multi-Purpose Spray Lube; from garage-doors-and-parts.com). Also hit the torsion bar bearings, the opener track and any other pivot points. The special lube penetrates the

GARAGE DOOR LUBE

1 Snug up all the nuts and bolts on your garage door and check for worn parts and replace where needed. Then spray all the moving components with garage door lubricant.

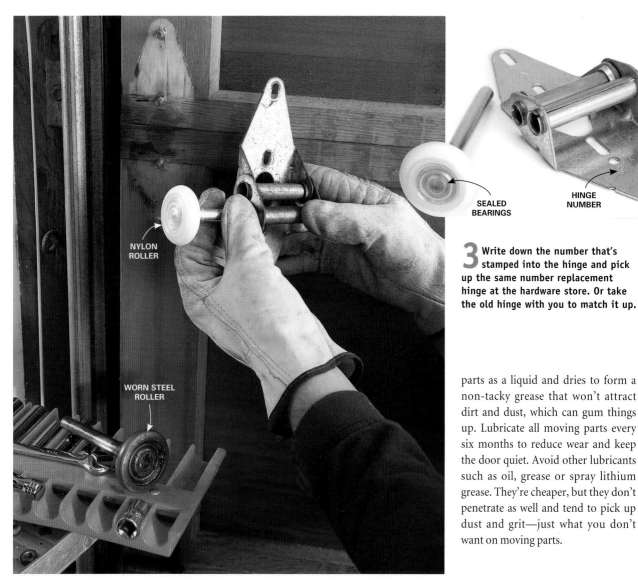

NYLON ROLLER

WORN STEEL ROLLER

SEALED BEARINGS

HINGE NUMBER

3 Write down the number that's stamped into the hinge and pick up the same number replacement hinge at the hardware store. Or take the old hinge with you to match it up.

parts as a liquid and dries to form a non-tacky grease that won't attract dirt and dust, which can gum things up. Lubricate all moving parts every six months to reduce wear and keep the door quiet. Avoid other lubricants such as oil, grease or spray lithium grease. They're cheaper, but they don't penetrate as well and tend to pick up dust and grit—just what you don't want on moving parts.

2 Replace the roller by unbolting the hinge and tilting the roller out of the track. Swap out the rollers and reinstall the hinge.

Car door protector

Protect your car doors and garage walls with a plush carpet remnant. Mount the carpet to your garage wall with adhesive-backed hook-and-loop fasteners such as Velcro.

One-day
workbench

L ike a traditional woodworker's bench, this workbench offers a large, rock-solid work surface and plenty of storage space below. But because it's built mostly from ready-made components, constructing this bench doesn't take much time or skill. If you have a little experience with simple hand and power tools, you can complete it in an afternoon.

You'll find everything you need for this project at home centers. You can use any combination of cabinets that add up to a width of less than 80 in. (the length of the door used for

the top). Shown here is a 60-in. sink base cabinet and an 18-in. drawer unit. Buy a solid-core door rather than a flimsy hollow-core door for the top. Although the cabinets shown here are oak, a mahogany (lauan) door was used. You can save some money if you choose unfinished rather than prefinished cabinets, and construction-grade plywood rather than oak for the back. It won't be cheap either way, but you'd have to spend at least twice as much to buy a ready-made workbench of comparable size, storage capacity and durability.

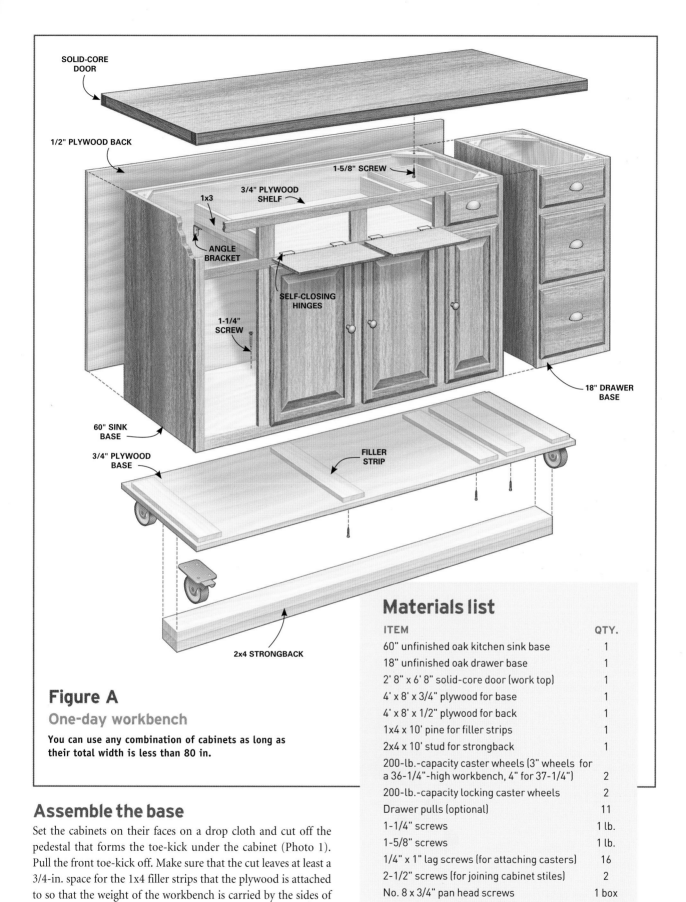

SOLID-CORE DOOR

1/2" PLYWOOD BACK

1-5/8" SCREW

3/4" PLYWOOD SHELF

1x3

ANGLE BRACKET

SELF-CLOSING HINGES

1-1/4" SCREW

60" SINK BASE

3/4" PLYWOOD BASE

FILLER STRIP

18" DRAWER BASE

2x4 STRONGBACK

Figure A
One-day workbench

You can use any combination of cabinets as long as their total width is less than 80 in.

Materials list

ITEM	QTY.
60" unfinished oak kitchen sink base	1
18" unfinished oak drawer base	1
2' 8" x 6' 8" solid-core door (work top)	1
4' x 8' x 3/4" plywood for base	1
4' x 8' x 1/2" plywood for back	1
1x4 x 10' pine for filler strips	1
2x4 x 10' stud for strongback	1
200-lb.-capacity caster wheels (3" wheels for a 36-1/4"-high workbench, 4" for 37-1/4")	2
200-lb.-capacity locking caster wheels	2
Drawer pulls (optional)	11
1-1/4" screws	1 lb.
1-5/8" screws	1 lb.
1/4" x 1" lag screws (for attaching casters)	16
2-1/2" screws (for joining cabinet stiles)	2
No. 8 x 3/4" pan head screws	1 box
Self-closing cabinet hinges	2 sets
1-1/2" angle brackets	8

Assemble the base

Set the cabinets on their faces on a drop cloth and cut off the pedestal that forms the toe-kick under the cabinet (Photo 1). Pull the front toe-kick off. Make sure that the cut leaves at least a 3/4-in. space for the 1x4 filler strips that the plywood is attached to so that the weight of the workbench is carried by the sides of the cabinets.

Lay the door on cardboard or a drop cloth and set the two cabinets upside down on top of it so you can join them on a

1 Cut the back and sides of the cabinet to remove the pedestal under the cabinet box. Break off the toe-kick beneath the front of the cabinet.

2 Align the cabinets and screw their face frames together. The door you'll use for the top provides a perfectly flat surface to set the cabinets on.

perfectly flat surface. Shim any low spots under the door so it stays flat. Attach the filler strips under the cabinets, predrilling and screwing up through the base with 1-1/4-in. screws (see Figure A). Align the cabinet stiles, then screw the cabinets together with 2-1/2-in. screws at the top and bottom (Photo 2).

Use a shim and a clamp to hold the cabinet sides parallel (see Photo 2). Cut a 3/4-in. plywood base the same length as the assembled cabinets but 1/2 in. wider. Mount the base flush with the front of the cabinets and overhanging the back by 1/2 in. (This provides a lip for the back to rest on.) Predrill and screw on the casters with lag screws 1 in. back from the edges, placing the locking wheels in front. Glue and screw two 2x4s to the plywood behind the farthest turn of the front wheels to keep the center of the workbench from sagging (Photo 3).

Tip the base upright and lock the wheels. Set the plywood back on the base's lip (Photo 4) and fasten it to the cabinets with 3/4-in. pan head screws from inside (cabinets with thicker backs may require a different size screw). The plywood back strengthens the workbench and provides a base for shelving and hooks.

Add the top

Set the solid-core door on top of the base. Center the door from side to side, then leave a 1-1/2-in. overhang in front to create an edge for clamping.

Attach the top at the corner braces (Photo 5). Screw on additional angle brackets to the front and back if needed for more strength.

Sand any rough edges on the door, then add shelves to

Off-the-shelf components make it easy

This workbench is made from two store-bought base cabinets mounted on casters and topped off with a solid-core door. To build it, all you need are the materials shown here. But don't let the simple construction fool you; this is a heavy-duty workbench that will stand up to decades of use.

SOLID-CORE DOOR

STOCK CABINET

the sides and back. If you need to compensate for an uneven garage floor, jam shims or wedges under the bench after you roll it into position.

3 Screw a plywood base to the undersides of the cabinets and add a double 2x4 "strongback" to prevent the workbench from sagging in the middle.

STRONGBACK

4 Glue and screw a plywood back to the cabinets. The back strengthens the workbench and provides a fastener surface for shelves, hooks or other hardware.

5 Fasten the top with screws only—no glue. After years of wear, you can simply flip the top over to get a flawless new work surface.

Save money with a sink cabinet

A 60-in. sink base cabinet was chosen for this project because it cost less than two 30-in. cabinets. The downside of a sink base is that it has false drawer fronts instead of drawers. To make use of that space, install a shelf in the cabinet and mount the drawer fronts on hinges. This creates a perfect cubbyhole for bar clamps and other long tools. Mark the drawer front positions with tape before you remove the fronts and attach the hinges.

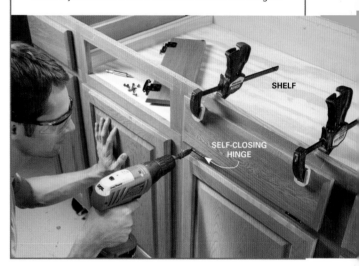

SHELF

SELF-CLOSING HINGE

Angle-iron tool slots

Screw a length of leftover slotted angle iron to the side of your workbench to keep tools at hand. The slots work especially well for screwdrivers and wrenches.

1-1/2" x 1-1/2" ANGLE

Try this! Garage spruce-ups

Parking mat

It's one thing to get dirt on your garage floor, but when your vehicle drips motor oil, transmission fluid, rain and melting snow, you can end up with a real mess and an ugly stain. It's even worse when you get it on your shoes and track it into the house. The solution? Park your vehicle on a giant mat.

The Clean Park Garage Mat is made with 20- or 50-mil vinyl, similar to a pool liner, to protect garage floors from tire tracks and dripping fluids. The raised 1-in. snap-on bracket edges contain water and slush.

allmats.com

VINYL MAT

SNAP-ON BRACKETS

DIY garage floor coating kit

Want a showroom-quality garage floor without the hefty price tag? One garage floor coating option is RockSolid's professional-grade, one-day, three-coat DIY polyurea coating kit. Polyurea has been used in commercial coating applications for 25 years. It forms a UV-stable and flexible protective shell that allows for the natural expansion and contraction of concrete without cracking. It resists road salt, chemicals, and the peeling, chipping or lifting from hot tires that can sometimes occur with garage floor coatings. Rock Solid's polyurea coating is low odor and, according to the manufacturer, cures so fast you can finish coating your garage floor in one day and drive on it the next.

rocksolidfloors.com

RockSolid Floors

Agri Products (3)

Turn your garage into a screen room, option I

Are pesky mosquitoes and other bugs keeping you from tinkering in your garage? Take back your workshop by putting a huge screen door over the opening. Shown here is the Power Remote Door Screen. The side rails and screen form a tight seal, locking out pests. The lower-cost Easy Crank Screen substitutes a hand crank for the motor. Or you can go for the Snap On Screen, which snaps on and off any door frame or opening and is even less expensive. The systems are available online.

durascreens.com

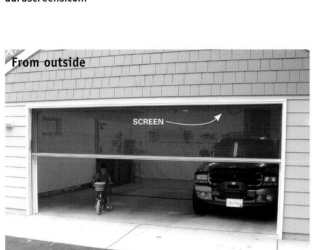

From outside

From inside

Add curb appeal with a new garage door

A new garage door may be the quickest way to give the exterior of your house a face-lift. Often the largest and most prominent feature of a home, a garage door that's tailor-made can make a highly visible improvement. And Clopay makes choosing the right door a breeze with its Door Imagination System, which lets you upload a photo of your house and plug in any door style, hardware option and window configuration you can dream up. The door styles range from old-fashioned carriage house doors to modern translucent ones like the door shown here.

Clopay makes doors with real and faux wood, steel and composite, and in a variety of colors and stains and finishes. If good looks aren't enough of an excuse for a new door, energy efficiency may be. Certain insulated Clopay models provide an R-value of 20. As you might guess, the prices of these doors vary considerably. A single-stall stamped metal door can run as little as $350, or you could pay more than $10,000 for a door with fancy features.

Turn your garage into a screen room, option 2

We've seen several versions of garage door screens that fit over the opening to keep out bugs, but none with Fresh Air Screens' great prices. Installation only takes about 15 minutes. Nail the screen along the top (to the outside of the garage door frame so it won't interfere with the garage door), then use the hook-and-loop straps to adhere the frame along the sides and attach the screen. Slide a 3/4-in. plastic pipe or conduit (not included) through the pocket at the bottom of the screen to keep it rigid.

When you want the screen up, simply detach the sides, roll them up, and then fasten the straps along the top. It's a practical, inexpensive way to work in the garage without battling insects. Buy the screens at home centers or directly from the manufacturer.

www.freshairscreens.com

ZIPPER

Garage parking guide

If you want to know when to stop your vehicle in the garage, put this polyethylene mat on the floor where your front wheel sits. You'll feel a bump when you drive over it, letting you know when to stop. The mats, like this one from Racor, can be used for all types of cars and trucks.

racorinc.com

PARKING MAT

Racor

5

Quick fixes

Every homeowner has an internal list of things that need fixing around the house. Why is it so hard to get those little projects done? Here you'll find complete, simple how-to information for fixing stair squeaks, drafty doors, plugged-up drains, drippy faucets, damaged flooring and worn-out windows. You can knock off a chunk of your to-do list in one morning!

If the lighting in your home is uninspired, check out four upgrades you can do—no electrician required.

SPECIAL SECTION:
Easy lighting upgrades

Stop stair squeaks

Squeaky stairs are easy to fix from underneath—provided they're exposed. A simple fix is to tap shims into voids between the treads and the stringers and add some glue. Then screw the stringer to each stud. But most stairs are finished on the underside with drywall or plaster. Squeaks in these stairs need to be fixed from the top. That's why the perfect time to fix them is when you're replacing the carpeting—you can remove the treads and get at the squeaky culprits. (If you're not replacing the carpet, but you have a squeak that's driving you nuts, see p. 87 for how to fix tread squeaks right through the carpeting.) Here are four easy steps to permanently fix the treads that squeak and keep the rest from ever starting.

After you've removed the carpet, use a flat bar to pry off the treads, working from the top down (Photo 1). Since you'll be

FLAT BAR

1 Pry off each tread with a flat bar. Remove the nails and clean off any carpet pad or staples.

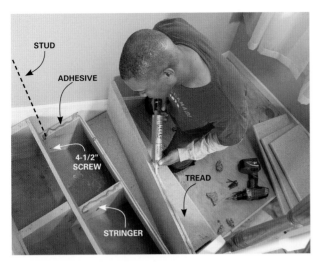

2 Apply a bead of subfloor adhesive along the top of the riser, the stringers and the back of the tread. Press the tread back into place.

3 Drive three 2-1/2-in. screws through the top of the tread into each stringer.

reusing the treads, remove the nails and any leftover carpet pad and staples. Screw the outside stringers to each stud with 4-1/2-in. screws (Photo 2). Starting with the bottom tread, apply a bead of subfloor adhesive (two brands are PL 400 and Liquid Nails) along the top of the riser, the stringers and the back of the tread, and press the tread back into place. Next, drive three 2-1/2-in. screws through the top of the same tread into each stringer (Photo 3). Then, drive a 2-in. screw through the riser into the back of the tread between the stringers (Photo 4). Repeat these steps with each tread, working your way to the top of the stairs.

Note: Your stairs will be out of commission for a couple of hours, so let everyone in the house know what's going on. Make sure you cordon off the top to keep someone from tumbling down the steps while you're working!

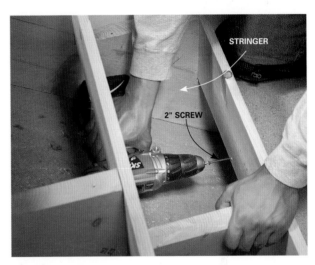

4 Drive a 2-in. screw through the riser into the back of the tread.

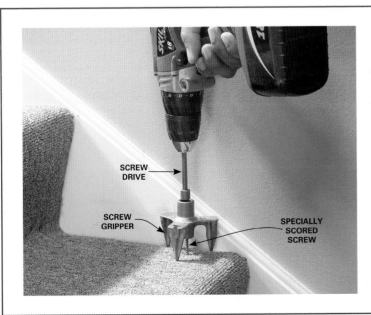

Fix squeaks through carpet

If you have carpeted stairs and a squeaky step that's driving you crazy, try the Squeeeeek No More kit (123itsdone.com). The kit is designed to send a snap-off screw right through the carpet without damaging the fibers. Find the squeak by bouncing up and down on each step, then drive the specially scored screw through the middle of the depth control jig, down through the carpeted tread, and into the stringer or riser nearest the squeak. The jig stops the screw head right below the tread's surface. Use the screw gripper located on one side of the jig to rock the screw back and forth until the excess length snaps off.

1 "Unzip" the old, damaged weather stripping, pulling it through the brad nails that hold it in.

Stop drafts
around doors

With heating costs going through the roof, here's an easy way to keep heat from slipping out your doors, too. Take 30 minutes and replace the weather stripping and door sweeps around your steel entry doors. Plan to do this project on a warm day since you'll have to remove the doors. Steel doors use a compression-style strip for the hinge side and a magnetic one for the knob side and the top. But look at the door and confirm the style of weather stripping on all three sides and the type of door sweep before you head to the store. You'll find replacement weather stripping and sweeps in a variety of lengths and colors at home centers and hardware stores.

To remove the door, close it and use a hammer and a pin punch or a thin nail to tap out the door hinge pins. Turn the knob, open the door slightly and lift it off the hinges. When you rip out the old weather stripping, you might find that it's tacked into place with small brad nails from the manufacturer. Leave

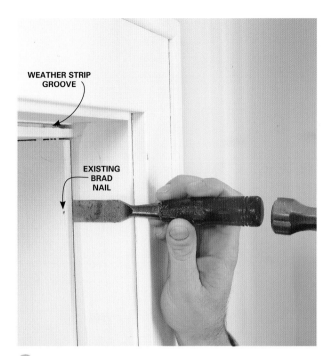

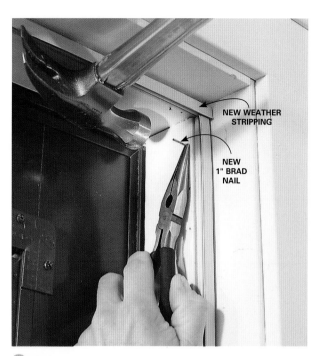

2 Cut off the old brad nails or push them all the way back into the groove with an old chisel.

3 Cut the new weather stripping to length and reinstall it, pinning it with new brad nails positioned near the old ones.

4 Peel out the old door sweep and caulk the ends of the door frame. Tap in the replacement sweep and staple the ends with 1/2-in. staples or the fasteners provided with the sweep.

5 Adjust the door threshold with a Phillips screwdriver. Move it up or down until the door closes smoothly with no light seeping through.

them in place after removing the old weather stripping or you'll damage the doorjamb. Then shear off the shanks inside the groove with an old chisel (Photo 2) or drive them deeper into the groove with a screwdriver. Press the new magnetic weather stripping firmly into the groove on the knob side and top of the door frame and do the same with the compression strip along the hinge side. To ensure that the strips won't pull out, pin them with a few 1-in. brad nails, especially in the magnetic strips (Photo 3).

The sweep on the door bottom is even easier to replace. Pry or slide out the old sweep. Run a bead of caulk along the bottom edge of the door, tap the sweep into place and then staple it at the ends (Photo 4). While you're at it, you might as well do a quick fine-tune of the adjustable threshold. Adjust all four screws until the door opens and closes without too much drag and any drafts have been eliminated (look for light between the sweep and the threshold with the door closed). Turn the screws clockwise to lower the threshold and counterclockwise to raise it (Photo 5).

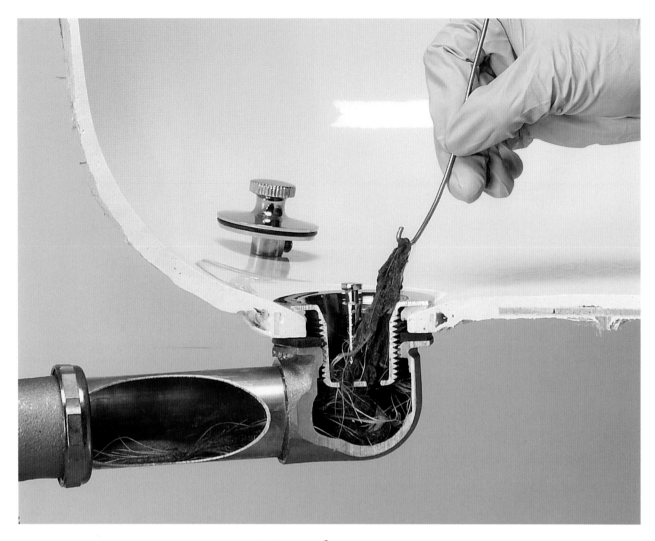

Unclog a
tub drain

About 80 percent of the time, you can fix slow-draining or clogged tub drains in five minutes, without chemicals and without a bill from a plumber. In most cases, you'll only need a screwdriver and a stiff wire or a bent coat hanger. The problem is usually just a sticky wad of hair that collects on the crossbars, a few inches under the stopper. All you need to do is figure out how to remove the stopper (that's almost always easy) and fish out the gunk. Bend a little hook on the end of the stiff wire with needle-nose pliers and shove it through the clog—you'll nearly always extract the entire ugly mess. If hair is wrapped around the crossbars, slice through it with a utility knife and then grab it with the wire.

Follow these photos to determine which type of stopper you have and how to remove it. The most common type, a drop stopper (shown at right), has a setscrew located under the cap.

Drop stoppers

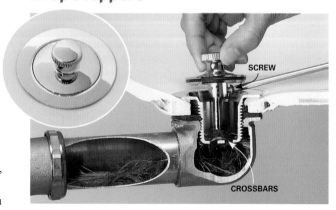

Lift the stopper and loosen the screw on the shaft slightly. Slide the stopper off the shaft.

Push/lock drain stoppers

These stoppers lock and seal when you press them down and release when you push down a second time. The way to remove them isn't so obvious. In most cases you have to hold the stem while unscrewing the cap as shown. With the cap off, you can sometimes fish out the hair from the crossbars. Otherwise simply remove the entire shaft by unscrewing it. You may have to adjust the screw tension on the stem when you reinstall everything to get a good seal.

Hold the stopper shaft tightly with a finger and unscrew the top.

Levered stoppers

Many tubs, certainly most older ones, have a stopper located inside the drain and overflow tube. Most of these have a lever on the overflow plate and a screen over the drain. The screen keeps most hair out of the drain, but some gets through and eventually forms a clog at the crossbars. Simply unscrew the screen for easy access to this clog and remove it. If the drain has an internal stopper, simply unscrew the overflow plate and pull the linkage and stopper up and out. Then clean the linkage and stopper and run water down the drain to flush it out.

Occasionally the linkage is out of adjustment and the stopper doesn't open far enough from its seat to allow a good flow. Adjust it, reinsert it and test it. Run water into the tub. If it leaks out, lengthen the stopper linkage to seal the drain better. If the drain doesn't open to let the water out, shorten the stopper linkage.

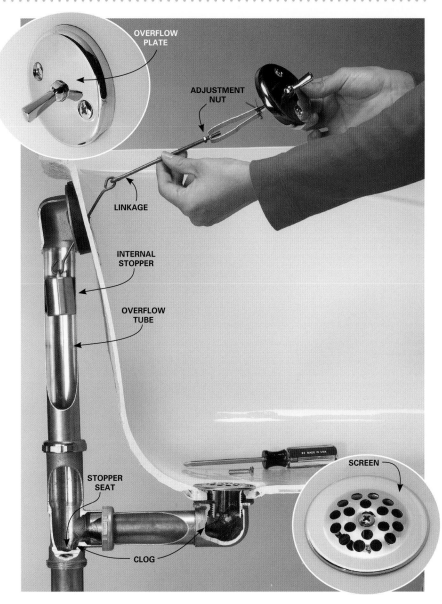

First remove the screen and clean the crossbars. Then unscrew the overflow plate, pull out the linkage, clean the stopper and linkage, and rinse the drainpipes. Readjust the linkage if necessary. Reinstall the assembly.

Fix a
ball-type faucet

When your single-lever, ball-type faucet starts dripping, it's time to replace the parts inside. You'll know you have a ball-type faucet (vs. a cartridge type) if it has a dome-shape cap under the handle (Figure A). This is an easy repair. Once you have the parts, the whole thing will take about 45 minutes and you'll save a good amount by doing it yourself!

Everything you need is available in a repair kit (found at home centers). Most kits include the ball, springs, seats, O-rings and an

Allen wrench. You'll also need to pick up faucet grease. There are several different models and types of ball-style faucets, so first follow our instructions to take apart your faucet. Then note the brand and take the old faucet guts along to the store to make sure you buy the right repair kit.

Before you disassemble your old faucet, turn off the water at the fixture shutoff valves under the

Figure A
Faucet

HANDLE

HANDLE SCREW

DECORATIVE SCREW COVER

CAP WITH ADJUSTING RING

COMBINATION CAM AND SEAL

STAINLESS STEEL BALL

SEATS

SPRINGS

SPOUT

O-RINGS

BODY

SPRAYER DIVERTER

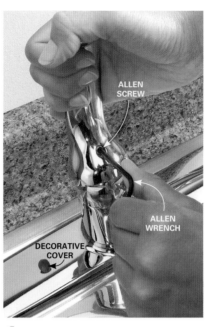

ALLEN SCREW

ALLEN WRENCH

DECORATIVE COVER

1 Lift the handle, pry off the decorative cover with your fingernail or a flat-blade screwdriver, then loosen the Allen screw underneath and lift the handle free.

ADJUSTING RING

OLD-STYLE CAM

TAB

SLOT

CAM SEAL

NEW-STYLE COMBINATION CAM & SEAL

2 Unscrew the cap under the handle and lift out the cam seal. Make sure to line up the tab on the cam seal with the slot on the faucet body when reassembling.

STAINLESS STEEL BALL

SLOT

PIN

3 Lift out the ball. When you put the faucet back together, line up the long slot on the side of the ball with the pin inside the faucet body.

sink or your home's main water valve if the individual shutoffs are missing (now is a good time to install some!). Cover the sink drain hole with a rag to avoid losing small parts down the drain.

The only tricky part of this repair is first locating and then loosening the Allen setscrew (see Photo 1) that anchors the handle to the stem. The screw is typically hidden under the decorative cover. If the faucet is old, you'll have to use some force with the Allen wrench to loosen the screw.

Your repair kit may include two different versions of the same part, one for newer and one for older-model faucets. It's best to use the same version as the existing parts and discard the other versions when you have the option. Most repair kits come with a hollow stainless steel ball. This will work

Repair kit contents

1. Old-style cam and seal
2. Combination cam and seal
3. Stainless steel ball
4. Old-style seats and springs
5. New-style seats and springs
6. Allen wrench
7. Different thickness O-rings

4 **Remove both sets of seats and springs. When you reassemble the faucet using newer-style springs, guide the seats and springs into the hole with the narrow end of the spring facing up (see Figure A).**

5 **Wiggle the spout free and remove it, and then slip out the O-rings. Pick matching sized O-rings from the kit, coat them with faucet grease and slide them on. Reassemble the faucet by following the disassembly steps in reverse.**

well and last longer than the original plastic ball you might find if yours is an older faucet. If your faucet uses an older-style, two-part cam—the plastic cam and a separate cam seal—and your kit comes with only the newer combined version (see Photo 2), go ahead and use the combined version. Just make sure to discard the existing adjusting ring located in the cap of your faucet or the handle won't fit correctly when you reassemble it.

Patch damaged vinyl flooring

You don't have to live with unsightly holes, burns or worn-out spots in your vinyl floor. If you can find a hidden spot on the same floor to steal a little flooring from, you can cut out the damaged area and make a nearly invisible patch.

Inside closets and under appliances are good places to look for matching flooring. Or, if you're really lucky, you'll find some scraps left behind by the flooring installer. The replacement piece should match the pattern of the damaged one and extend about 1/2 in. beyond these pattern lines. Keep in mind that the patch will be less conspicuous if you make the seams along grout lines or other divisions in the pattern. With a utility knife, cut a square from the floor in a hidden location. Loosen the adhesive in one corner with a hair dryer and lift the corner with a putty knife. Then work the piece loose by applying heat to the old adhesive while gently pulling up the vinyl (Photo 1).

To install the patch, you'll need vinyl flooring adhesive, a 1/16-in. notched trowel or notched putty knife for spreading the adhesive, and a seam-sealing kit. You'll find all these items at home centers or flooring stores. Patch the floor as shown in Photos 2 and 3. Follow the instructions on the label for spreading and drying time. Finish up by applying seam sealer according to the kit instructions.

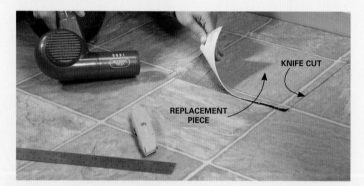

1 **Cut out a piece of flooring from an inconspicuous place. Make sure the piece you cut out has a pattern that matches the piece you'll replace.**

2 **Tape the replacement piece over the damaged section. Cut through both pieces with a sharp utility knife, following grout or pattern lines. Keep the blade straight up and down.**

3 **Remove the damaged section of flooring and any backing material that may be stuck to the floor. Glue in the replacement section and seal the seam with vinyl-floor seam sealer.**

Easy carpet fixes

Get pro results— without the pro price

The carpet in your home is a big investment. So it's frustrating when a sputtering ember from the fireplace burns a hole in your beautiful rug or a spring storm floods the basement family room. But you don't have to call in a pro or just live with the damage until you replace the carpet. Solving these problems yourself isn't difficult, and you can increase the life of your carpet and save some real money.

Here you'll learn how to fix three common problems:

- Carpet that has pulled out of a metal threshold
- Small damaged spots such as holes, tears or burns
- Wet carpet from leaks or flooding

The tools and materials you'll need for these repairs are available at home centers.

Patch a damaged spot

Rescue wet carpet

Reattach pulled-out carpet

1 Part the carpet fibers with a Phillips screwdriver. The parts mark your cutting lines and let you cut the backing without cutting or tearing the fibers.

2 Cut through the carpet backing. Make the cuts as straight as you can and avoid cutting completely through the carpet pad.

Patch a damaged spot

You can patch a small hole, tear or burn using techniques that will make the repair virtually invisible. You'll need a small "plug" of carpet that matches the damaged piece. If you don't have a remnant, you can steal a piece from inside a closet or underneath a piece of furniture you never intend to move. (This may sound extreme, but it's a lot cheaper than replacing the entire carpet.)

If you have a "plush"-type carpet with a flat surface and no pattern, you can make a repair that's absolutely invisible. If your carpet has a color pattern, a textured surface design or looped yarn, you'll have to be fussier when you cut the plug, and the repair may be visible (but you're probably the only one who will notice it).

Before starting this repair, buy a carpet knife that has replaceable blades. You'll also need a roll of one-sided carpet tape. Be sure to choose heavy-duty tape reinforced with mesh, not the thin, flimsy version or the "hot-melt" type that requires a special iron to apply.

A carpet knife makes straighter, cleaner cuts than a utility knife.

Cut out the damage and a matching plug

Be sure the area you're working in is well lit. To mark the area you'll cut out, part the carpet fibers around the damage as if you were parting your hair

(Photo 1). Keep the part lines at least 1/2 in. from the damaged spot. Cut along the parts using a sharp, new blade in your carpet knife (Photo 2).

Next, cut a replacement plug, using the cutout as a template. To start, make a first cut in the replacement material, using a straightedge to guide your carpet knife. Then set the cutout on the replacement material with one edge aligned along that first cut. When you lay the cutout on top of the replacement material, make sure their naps are running in the same direction. You can tell which direction the nap is running by rubbing your hand over the carpeting and watching which way the fibers fall or stand up. Once you have the cutout lined up correctly, part the fibers around the three uncut sides just as you did before.

Cut along the parts and test-fit the plug in the cutout hole, making sure the nap of the plug matches the nap of the surrounding carpet. If the plug is a little too big, trim off a single row of fibers with sharp scissors (old, dull scissors will tear the fibers).

Prepare the hole for the new plug

Cut pieces of carpet tape and position them in the hole without removing the backing (Photo 3). Cut the ends of the tape diagonally so the pieces will frame the hole without overlapping. The tricky part is getting the tape positioned so it's halfway under the plug and halfway under the surrounding carpet. A helper makes this easier.

After marking their positions in the hole, remove the pieces from the hole and carefully (this is sticky stuff!) remove the protective backing from the tape. While pulling the carpeting up with one hand, slip the tape pieces back into the prepared hole

CARPET TAPE

3 Test-fit all the pieces of carpet tape before you stick them in place permanently. Mark a square on the carpet pad to help align each piece later.

4 Peel off the tape's backing and set each piece in place, sticky side up. Don't let the super-sticky tape touch the carpet backing—or anything else—until it's in position.

one piece at a time (Photo 4). Be sure the edges of the tape line up with your markings.

Insert the plug

Now you're ready to fit the new plug into the hole. Pull the fibers of the surrounding carpet back from the edges. Push one side of the plug lightly onto the tape to make sure it's set exactly right—you really only have one shot at this (Photo 5). After you're sure the plug is placed correctly, use your fingers to work in the direction of the nap all the way around the hole as you press the plug down firmly onto each side of the tape.

A carpet tractor will do the best job of meshing the fibers, but a seam roller or even a rolling pin would work too. Place a large, heavy book on top of the plug overnight. Trim any fibers sticking up with sharp scissors. You'll be surprised how "invisible" this repair is once you're finished. You can vacuum and clean your carpeting as you normally would, and this repair should last as long as your carpet does.

5 Set the plug tightly against one side of the hole. Then lower the other edges into place, holding back the surrounding fibers. Press the plug into the tape with your fingers, then with a carpet tractor.

A carpet tractor will mesh the fibers and make the repair invisible.

Rescue wet carpet

A floor scraper is the best tool for removing old adhesive or staples.

When carpet gets soaked, you have to act fast. The longer it stays soggy, the more likely it is to stretch out, discolor or get moldy. If a large area is waterlogged, complete replacement may be the best option. But if only a corner or a small room is soaked, you can save the carpet with just a couple of hours of work.

Tear out the soggy pad

First, go to the corner nearest the wet area, grab the carpet with pliers and pull the carpet off the tack strip. Continue pulling the carpet off the tack strip by hand until you can fold back the entire wet section. Run a fan or two to dry the carpet.

Wet carpet pad is like a big sponge. You have to get rid of it ASAP. Cut around the wet area with a utility knife. Make straight cuts so you have straight seams when you patch in the new pad. If the pad is glued to a concrete floor, scrape it up with a floor scraper (Photo 1). If the pad is stapled to a wood subfloor, just pull up chunks of pad and pry or pull out the staples if you have just a few. For faster removal on a larger area, use a floor scraper. Have garbage bags handy to prevent drips on the carpeting. Wet pad is heavy. Don't fill the bags so full that you can't haul them out without wrecking your back!

Wipe up any water on the floor, then flop the wet carpet back into place. Drying it flat and in place helps the carpet retain its shape. Run fans until the floor and carpet are completely dry. This can take a couple of days.

Patch in the new pad

Measure the area of pad you need to replace and take a piece of the old pad to a flooring store or home center to find similar replacement pad. The color doesn't matter, but the new pad must be the same thickness and density as the old pad. Some stores will cut the pad to the size you need.

Fasten the pad to a concrete floor with carpet pad adhesive and duct-tape the seams together (Photo 2). On a wood subfloor, all you need is a staple gun and 5/16-in. staples. Use a utility knife to trim off any pad covering the tack strip.

Reattach the carpet

As you refasten the carpet to the tack strip, you need to stretch it toward the wall. If you're dealing with a corner or a small area, you can use a knee kicker alone (see Photo 3, p. 99). Starting at one end of the loose carpet, set the head of the kicker about 2 in. from the tack strip and nudge the carpet tight against the wall. Force the carpet into the tack strip with a stiff putty knife. Also tuck the edge of the carpet into the space between the wall and the tack strip with a putty knife. Continue along the wall, moving the kicker over about a few inches each time.

If you're dealing with a larger area of carpet or if the carpet has stretched out of shape, bubbled or wrinkled after getting wet, you'll need to rent a power stretcher to restretch the carpet (available by the day at tool rental centers).

CARPET ROLLED BACK

WET PAD

NEW PAD

CARPET PAD ADHESIVE

1 Dry out wet carpet right away. Fold back the carpet and start a fan. Cut around the soaked section of pad and scrape it up.

2 Lay replacement pad after the floor has dried. Duct-tape the seams where new pad meets old, and fasten the pad to the floor with adhesive or staples.

Reattach pulled-out carpet

If you have carpet that has pulled loose from a metal threshold, fix it now, before the exposed edge of the carpet begins to fray. If the damage extends more than an inch or so away from the threshold, you won't be able to make a good-looking repair. Aside from standard hand tools, you'll need a carpet knife and a knee kicker, which you can get at any rental center. You'll also need a new metal threshold of the appropriate length and 1-1/2-in. ring-shank drywall nails.

THRESHOLD

1 Bend open the threshold's lip to release the carpet. Be careful not to snag the carpet as you push the screwdriver under the lip.

2 Pry up the threshold just enough to raise the nail heads. Then pull the nails and remove the threshold. Work from the carpeted side to avoid scratching the hard flooring. Nail down a new threshold.

Remove the old threshold

This repair is much easier if you first remove the door. You can do it with the door in place, but it'll take a little longer and you risk scratching the door. Carefully pry up the lip of the existing metal threshold along its entire length using a screwdriver or flat pry bar (Photo 1). Since you'll be replacing the threshold, you don't have to worry about wrecking it, but you want to work carefully so you don't damage the carpet edge even more. Once the threshold lip is bent up, use pliers to gently pull the carpeting up from the teeth inside the threshold. Roll the carpet back slightly to get it out of the way (you can leave the carpet pad in place).

Pry up the threshold slightly and pull the nails (Photo 2). To get an exact measurement for cutting the new threshold, don't measure the old threshold because it may be kinked. Instead, measure the opening and then cut the threshold with metal snips or a hacksaw.

Install the new threshold

If the carpet edge is in good shape, you can place the new threshold exactly where the old one was. If the edge is badly frayed, you'll need to trim off the damage using a carpet knife and a straightedge. Then position the new threshold farther into the carpeted room to compensate for the width you trimmed off. In most cases, you can place the new threshold about 1 in. from the original position, but not more. If you've moved the threshold more than an inch, you may also need to trim the carpet pad so it doesn't cover the threshold pins.

If you're working on a wood subfloor, nail down the replacement threshold with 1-1/2-in. ring-shank drywall nails. On a concrete floor, use heavy-duty construction adhesive to glue the threshold to the floor, and allow a day for it to dry before moving on to the next step.

KNEE KICKER

3 Nudge the carpet toward the threshold with a rented "knee kicker" and force the carpet into the threshold's teeth with a stiff putty knife.

4 Drive down the lip, tapping gradually back and forth along its entire length. On the final pass, pound hard to lock the carpet into the threshold.

Attach the carpet

Now you're ready to attach the carpet to the new threshold. Starting at one end of the threshold, set the head of the knee kicker about 2 in. from the threshold and kick with your knee to stretch the carpet toward the threshold (Photo 3). Kick firmly, but not with all your strength or you might rip the carpet. Force the carpet into the threshold teeth with a stiff putty knife. Then move the kicker over a few inches (the width of the kicker's head) and repeat the process until you reach the other end of the threshold. When you're done, tuck any loose carpet under nearby baseboards with a stiff putty knife. Finally, pound down the threshold lip with a rubber mallet (Photo 4).

Make old windows *like* new

Don't replace casement windows—repair them

If you're thinking about replacing your casement windows because they're drafty, fogged up or just hard to open, consider this: You can fix most of the problems yourself for a fraction of the cost of new windows—and it won't take you more than an hour or two per window.

Here you'll learn the fixes for the most common casement window problems. (Casement windows are the type that swing like doors.) You won't need any specialty tools, and the materials are available from most window manufacturers or online window supply companies (see the Buyer's guide, p. 101).

Although your windows may look different from the ones shown here, the techniques for removing the sash and fixing problems are similar.

Replace a sagging hinge

Over time, hinge arms that support heavy windows can start to sag, causing the sash to hit the frame in the lower corner that's opposite the hinge. First make sure the window sash is square and centered in the window opening. If it's not, see "Fix a sticking window," p. 103. To eliminate drag in a window that fits squarely, replace the hinge arms at the top and the bottom of the window. You can buy the hinges at window hardware supply stores (see the Buyer's guide, p. 101; prices vary).

Remove the sash from the window. The hinge arms are located near a corner or in the middle of the window frame. Unscrew the hinge arms from the window, then install the new ones in the same locations (photo right).

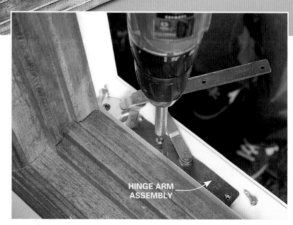

HINGE ARM ASSEMBLY

Align the new hinge arm with the screw holes and fasten it into place. If the screw holes are stripped out, fill them with toothpicks dipped in wood glue, let the glue dry, then cut the toothpicks flush.

Replace a stubborn crank operator

If the splines on the crank operator shaft are worn or broken off, the gears don't turn easily or at all, then it's time to replace the crank operator.

You don't need the make, model or serial number of the crank operator. You just need a picture. Snap a digital photo, email it to a hardware supply company (see the Buyer's guide) and the company will sell you a new one. You can also look at online catalogs at the sites listed below to find an operator that matches yours.

To replace the operator, first take the crank arm off the sash. Most crank arms slip out of a notch on the guide track on the sash (Photo 1). Others are pried off with a flathead screwdriver, or a channel is unscrewed from along the bottom of the sash. If the operator also contains a split arm operator, unhook that, too (Photo 2).

Slide or pry off the operator cover. If you have a removable cover, cut along the casement cover with a utility knife to slice through any paint or stain that seals it on the window jamb. Remove the trim screws along the top of the casement cover. Gently pry the cover loose (Photo 3). Be careful—the cover can easily break! Unscrew the crank operator. Set the new operator in place, aligning it with the existing screw holes, and screw it to the jamb. If the cover isn't removable, crank operator screws will be accessible on the exterior of the window.

1 Open the window until the crank arm bushing is aligned with the guide track notch. Push down on the arm to pop the bushing out of the track.

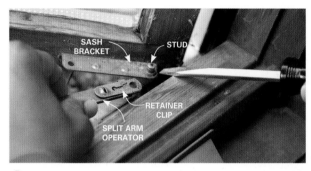

2 Slide back the retainer clip on the arm and pry the arm off the stud on the sash bracket with a screwdriver.

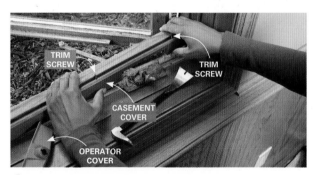

3 Lift off the casement cover to expose the crank operator. Remove the screws, take out the crank operator and replace it.

Figure A Casement window operation

When you turn the handle, the operator moves the crank arm and the split arm operator. The split arm operator then opens the window sash. Casement window operators come in several styles. They may look complex, but they're easy to disconnect, remove and replace.

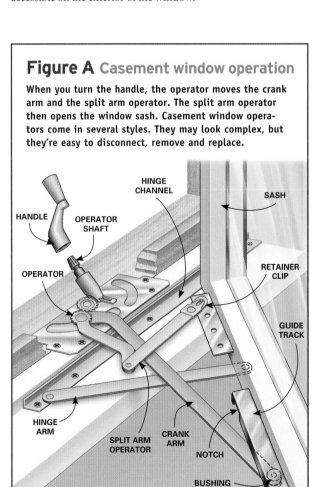

Buyer's guide

Blaine Window Hardware. Window hardware, including hard to find and obsolete hardware parts. Will find your replacement parts using your photos. blainewindow.com

Glass Distributors. Window hardware. glassdistributorsinc.com

Prime-Line Products. Replacement handles. prime-line-products.com

Strybuc Industries. Window hardware, including obsolete parts. strybuc.com

Truth Hardware. Window hardware. Refers homeowners to regional distributors, which can find parts using your photos. truth.com

Fix a stripped crank handle

If you turn your window handle and nothing happens, the gears on your handle, crank operator shaft or both are probably stripped. Take off the handle and look for signs of wear. If the teeth are worn, replace the handle (see the Buyer's guide, p. 101). If the shaft is worn, you can replace the whole operator (see p. 101). But here's a home remedy to try first.

Start by backing out the setscrew to remove the handle (some newer handles don't have setscrews and simply pull off—and this fix won't work). If you have a folding handle, mark where the setscrew is on the operator shaft when the window is closed and the handle is folded up. Remove the handle and file the shaft so the setscrew can lock onto the shaft (photo right). The metal is tough; it'll take about 15 minutes to get a flat side. Or use a rotary tool with a grinder bit to speed up the job. Vacuum the shavings out of the operator so they won't harm the moving parts.

Reattach the handle with a longer setscrew (available at

File a flat spot on the operator shaft, then insert a longer setscrew into the handle. The flat side lets the setscrew lock onto the shaft.

hardware stores). If you open and close the window a lot, this fix may not hold up in the long run.

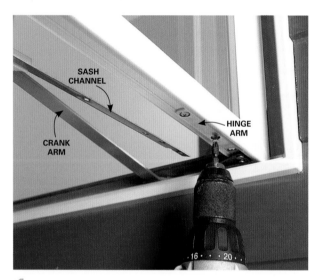

1 Take off the sash by removing the screws in the channel and the hinge arms. Then slide the sash off the hinge arms.

2 Align the sash lip with the hinge arms, then slide the sash onto the hinges. Insert screws to fasten the sash in place.

Replace a fogged sash

If you have broken glass or fogging (condensation between the glass panes), you'll have to replace the glass or the entire sash. If the sash is in good shape (not warped or cracked), you can sometimes replace just the glass. Contact your window manufacturer to see whether glass replacement is an option and if a fogged window is covered under your warranty. You'll need the information that's etched into the corner of the glass and the sash dimensions.

Contact a glass repair specialist to have only the glass replaced (search "Glass Repair" online). Or you can replace the sash

yourself. Order it through the manufacturer.

To replace the sash, first remove the old one. You take this sash off by removing the hinge screws (Photo 1). For sashes that slide out, see Photos 1 and 2, p. 103. Remove any hardware from the damaged sash and install it on the new sash (this sash doesn't require any hardware).

Install the new sash by sliding it onto the hinge arms, then screw it to the hinges (Photo 2).

1 Open the sash and disconnect the crank arm. Pry the split arm operator off the top and the bottom of the sash with a screwdriver (the hinge arms easily pop off).

2 Slide the hinge shoes out of the hinge channels at the top and bottom of the window to remove the sash.

Fix a sticking window

If you have a window that drags against the frame when you open it, close the window and examine it from the outside. The sash should fit squarely and be centered in the frame. If not, you can adjust the position of the sash by slightly moving the hinge channel. (If the window is centered and square but still drags, see "Replace a sagging hinge," p. 100.)

You can move the channel at the top or the bottom of the window, depending on where the sash is dragging (but don't move both channels). Start by taking out the sash (Photos 1 and 2). If the hinge arm is screwed to the sash, see Photo 1, p. 102.

Mark the hinge channel location on the frame, then unscrew the channel. Fill the screw holes with epoxy (for vinyl windows) or wood filler (for wood windows). Filling the holes keeps the screws from realigning with their old locations when you reinstall the channel. Scrape the filled holes smooth before the epoxy sets. Place the channel back on the jamb, about 1/8 in. over from the mark (move the channel away from the side of the sash that's dragging), drill 1/8-in. pilot holes and then reinstall it (Photo 3).

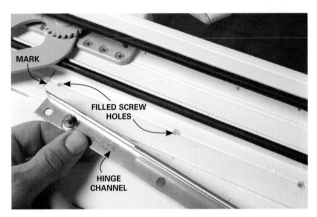

3 Set the hinge channel in place, slightly over from its former location. Drill new holes, then screw it to the jamb.

Is the window "glued" shut?

If the window is stuck shut, it's likely that the weather strip is sticking. After you muscle it open, spray silicone lubricant on a rag and wipe it on the weather stripping. Don't use oily lubricants; they attract dust.

Seal a drafty window

Weather stripping often becomes loose, worn or distorted when the sash drags or when the strip gets sticky and attaches itself to the frame, then pulls loose when the sash is opened. Windows have weather strip on the sash, frame or both. Regardless of its location, the steps for removing and replacing it are the same. Weather stripping is available from your window manufacturer. The window brand and glass manufacturer date are etched in the corner of the glass or in the aluminum spacer between the glass panes. You'll also need the height and width of your sash (take these measurements yourself).

If the weather strip is in good shape and loose in only a few places, like the corners, apply a dab of polyurethane sealant to the groove and press the weather strip into place. Otherwise, replace the entire weather strip. First remove the sash and set it on a work surface so you can access all four sides. If the weather strip is one continuous piece, cut it apart at the corners with a utility knife.

Starting at a corner, pull the weather strip loose from the sash (photo right). If the spline tears off and remains stuck in the groove, make a hook from stiff wire to dig it out.

Work the old weather strip out of the groove gently to avoid tearing it and leaving the spline stuck in the groove.

Work the new weather strip into the groove, starting at a corner. You'll hear it click as the strip slides into the groove.

From recessed to pendant in 5 minutes

Tired of your old recessed lights? Try Worth Home Products' new pendant lights. Installation is simple: Unscrew the recessed light, adjust the length of the pendant light cord, screw the adapter in, slide the canopy up to the ceiling and you have a new light hanging overhead. A room transformation doesn't get any easier than this (if you can change a lightbulb, you can install these lights).

worthhomeproducts.com

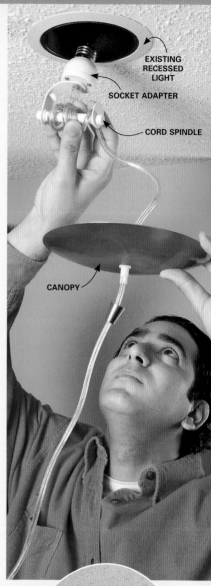

EXISTING RECESSED LIGHT

SOCKET ADAPTER

CORD SPINDLE

CANOPY

NEW PENDANT

Wireless switch upgrade

If you want to operate a chain-pull light with a wall switch, you can save the hassle of tearing into the walls and ceiling by installing a wireless wall switch. One option includes a screw-in radio receiver that installs between the porcelain fixture and the bulb. The battery-powered switch mounts on any wall. Although it's inexpensive, it's not very attractive and only powers a 60-watt incandescent bulb (it won't work with CFLs or enclosed fixtures).

If you plan to install an enclosed fixture or don't want to deal with dead batteries, buy a self-powered wireless switch kit (**smarthomeusa.com**) from econoswitch.com/kits. You can mount the wall switch anywhere on the wall as long as it's within 100 ft. of the receiver/relay.

Caution: Turn off the power before you install the receiver/relay.

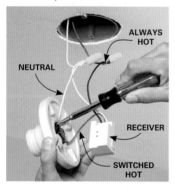

ALWAYS HOT

NEUTRAL

RECEIVER

SWITCHED HOT

1 Disconnect the black and white wires from the porcelain fixture (power off). Connect them to the receiver/relay black and white wires. Then connect the red and white wires from the relay to the fixture.

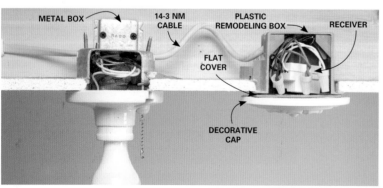

METAL BOX

14-3 NM CABLE

PLASTIC REMODELING BOX

RECEIVER

FLAT COVER

DECORATIVE CAP

2 If your pull chain fixture is mounted on a metal box, the receiver won't work because the metal will shield the radio signal. Either replace the box with a plastic one or mount a plastic remodeling box near it.

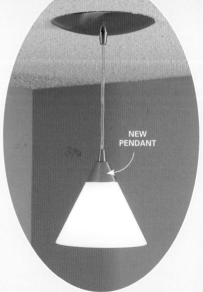

Update recessed lights

Renew those old recessed lights by replacing the baffle trim with a snazzier choice like an eyeball trim. It'll dress up your room and allow you to point the light to illuminate interesting objects or areas. Check with the supplier or manufacturer to determine if eyeball trim is available for your model of light canister (the canister should be labeled inside with the manufacturer, model, trim and lamps allowed).

Before starting, turn on the light, and then flip the circuit breaker off. When the light goes out, the power is off. Remove the old baffle trim as shown in Photo 1. If you don't have baffle trim, or it's different from that in the photo, the attachment system will vary slightly. Photo 2 shows how to free the light socket from its housing. (Socket-mounting systems also vary; your removal method may be different.) Connect the socket to the eyeball and secure the trim as shown in Photo 3.

Look inside the canister to find the maximum light bulb wattage. Eyeball trims require a special bulb, either a flood or reflector bulb (see photo at left) that directs light away from the canister.

REFLECTOR LIGHT BULB

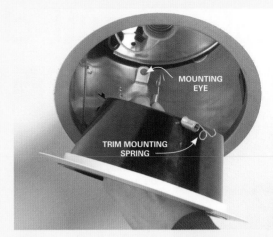

MOUNTING EYE

TRIM MOUNTING SPRING

1 Turn off the power and remove the light bulb. Reach up into the light canister and unhook both trim springs from their mounting eyes, and remove the trim.

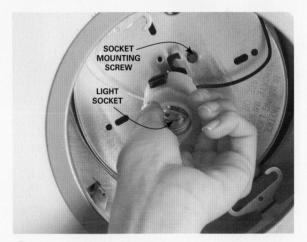

SOCKET MOUNTING SCREW

LIGHT SOCKET

2 Loosen the socket mounting screw enough to twist the socket loose and pull it free. Lightly tighten the mounting screw after the socket is freed.

Light fixture assistant

You don't need a third hand to hold up a ceiling fixture while you connect the wiring. Support the fixture with a scrap of wire wrapped around one of the mounting screws.

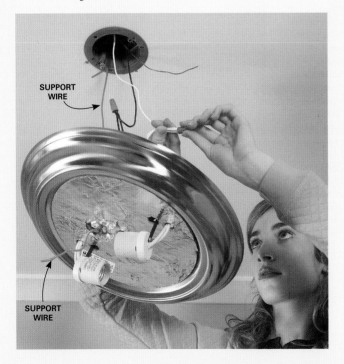

SUPPORT WIRE

SUPPORT WIRE

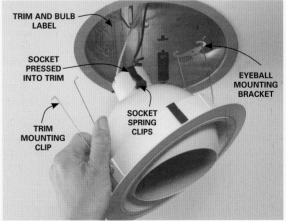

TRIM AND BULB LABEL

SOCKET PRESSED INTO TRIM

EYEBALL MOUNTING BRACKET

TRIM MOUNTING CLIP

SOCKET SPRING CLIPS

3 Squeeze the socket spring clips together and press the socket into the top of the new eyeball. Pinch the trim mounting clips together, insert them into the mounting brackets and push the trim tight to the ceiling.

Replace a pull-chain light fixture

1 Turn off the power, remove the light bulb and unscrew the fixture from the electrical box. Pull the fixture down, but keep your hands away from the wires. Touch one voltage tester probe to the black wire, and the other to the white wire. If the voltage indicator doesn't light up, the power is off.

> **CAUTION**
> Turn off power at the main panel.

TERMINAL SCREWS

BROKEN PULL SWITCH

Pull-chain light fixtures are handy for basements and storage areas—until they quit working. The internal switch mechanism can wear out, or pulling too hard on the cord can snap the chain or completely pull it out of the fixture. Replacing the broken fixture is simple and inexpensive (found at any home center or hardware store). Pull-chain fixtures are made from either plastic or porcelain, but we recommend the porcelain because it withstands heat better and lasts longer.

Before starting, flip the circuit breaker or pull the fuse to disconnect the power to the light, then test to make sure the power is off (Photo 1). Replace the broken fixture as shown in Photos 2 and 3. There may be an unused bare ground wire inside the electrical box. If it falls down while you're replacing the fixture, wrap it in a circle and push it up as far into the electrical box as possible.

> **CAUTION**
> Aluminum wiring requires special handling. If you have aluminum wiring, call in a licensed pro who's certified to work with it. This wiring is dull gray, not the dull orange that's characteristic of copper.

2 Loosen the terminal screws and unhook the wiring from the old fixture. If the wire ends are broken or corroded, strip off 3/4 in. of sheathing, and bend the bare wire end into a hook.

3 Attach the black wire to the gold terminal screw on the new fixture and the white wire to the silver terminal screw. Wrap the wires clockwise so they cover at least three-quarters of the terminal screws. Firmly tighten the screws so the copper wire compresses slightly. Twist the fixture to spiral the wires into the electrical box. Screw the new fixture to the box snugly, but don't overtighten it or the porcelain might crack.

GROUND WIRE

PUSH UP

WIRE WRAPPED AROUND THREE-FOURTHS OF SCREW

SILVER TERMINAL SCREW

GOLD TERMINAL SCREW

NEW PULL-CHAIN FIXTURE

CHAPTER

6

Fast furniture

Inexpensive discount-store furniture is fine, but it never seems to last. Rather than buying something you'll have to replace in a year or two, take the time you'd spend shopping and make that table, storage box or bench yourself! You don't need a shop full of specialty tools, and you'll find all of the materials at a home center. In a few hours, you can create something you'll be proud of and that will last for years instead of months.

Magazine stand

The magazine stand shown is made from Merbau, a tropical hardwood. You can substitute any hardwood. Aluminum tube was used to join the frame and flat bars to hang magazines. Get your wood before starting, and use 5/16-in. dowels to join the frame, with 3/8-in. dowels for a tight fit with the tube.

Cutting list

ITEM	QTY.	SIZE	ITEM	QTY.	SIZE
Hardwood			**Aluminum**		
Sides	2	39-1/4" x 3-1/2" x 3/4"	Flat bars	18	12-3/4" x 3/4" x 1/8"
Base	2	12" x 3-1/2" x 3/4"	Tube	6	12-1/4" x 1/2"
Rail	2	12-1/4" x 3-1/2" x 3/4"			

Figure A
Magazine stand

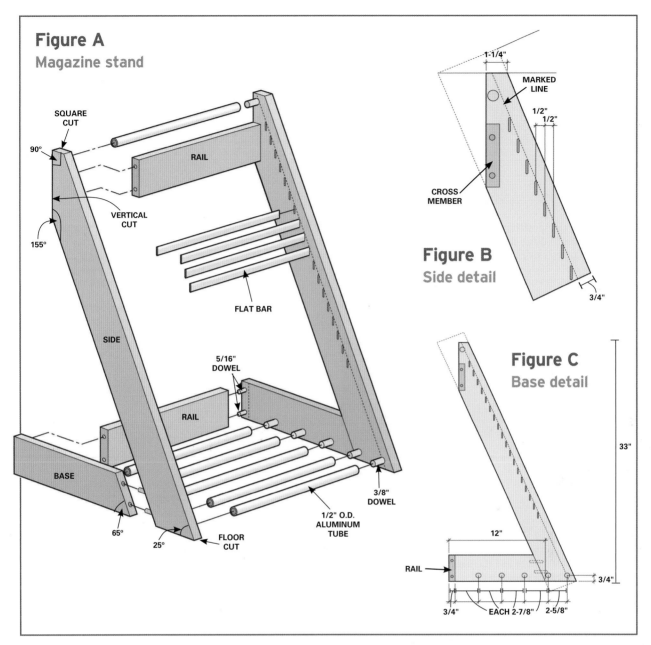

SQUARE CUT

90°

155°

65°

25°

RAIL

VERTICAL CUT

SIDE

BASE

RAIL

FLAT BAR

5/16" DOWEL

3/8" DOWEL

1/2" O.D. ALUMINUM TUBE

FLOOR CUT

Figure B
Side detail

1-1/4"

MARKED LINE

1/2"
1/2"

CROSS MEMBER

3/4"

Figure C
Base detail

33"

12"

RAIL

3/4"

3/4"   EACH 2-7/8"   2-5/8"

1 **Cut side and base ends.** Mark a 65-degree angle on the ends of the bases. On the sides, mark 25 degrees as the floor cut and 155 degrees as the vertical wall cut at the top (see Figure A), then cut with a sliding compound miter saw. Square-cut the top of the sides 1-1/4 in. wide.

2 **Mark the slot setback.** Set a marking gauge to 3/4 in. to scribe a setback line down the long inside front edges of the sides. Use this line as a guide for the beginning of each slot to house the aluminum flat bars.

MARKING GAUGE

3/4"

SETBACK LINE

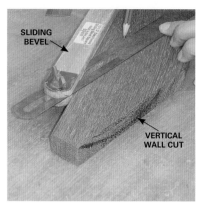

SLIDING BEVEL

VERTICAL WALL CUT

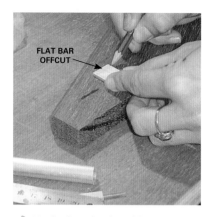

FLAT BAR OFFCUT

3 Mark the slot positions. Set a sliding bevel to match the 155-degree cut at the top. Beginning 1-1/2 in. from the top, mark 3/4-in.-long lines from the setback line. Measure down 1/2 in. to make the next mark, marking 18 slots in each side.

4 Mark slots in the sides. Cut a small piece of aluminum flat bar offcut as a template to mark the slot shapes on the sides, centering it on the vertical lines, against the setback line, to trace the shape (see Figure B).

5 Rout the slots. Clamp the sides to a workbench and use a clamped board set at the same angle as the slots as a jig to guide the router. Use a 1/8-in. bit to make 1/8-in.-wide x 1/2-in.-deep slots. TIP: Reverse the jig to make cuts on the opposite side piece.

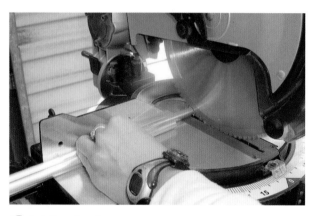

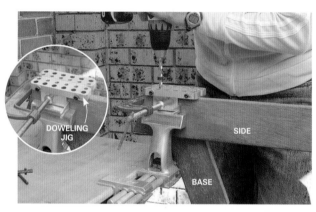

DOWELING JIG

SIDE

BASE

6 Cut the aluminum. Use a sliding compound miter saw to cut the aluminum tube and flat bar, lightly sanding the ends of each piece to remove burrs.

7 Drill dowel holes. Use a drill with a 5/16-in. bit and a doweling jig to make dowel holes in the front end of the base and back edge of the side. Drill corresponding holes in the rails, base and sides, drilling five holes for tube dowels on the base, 3/4 in. from the edge (see Figure C).

Finishing

Lightly sand and round over edges with 180-grit sandpaper. Wipe clean and finish with carnauba wax, or a clear polyurethane to bring out the natural wood color and grain.

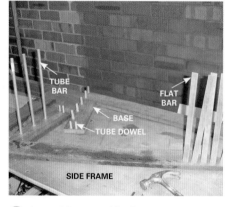

TUBE BAR

FLAT BAR

BASE

TUBE DOWEL

SIDE FRAME

8 Assemble one side frame. Secure the base to the side using glue and dowels. Secure the rails to the side frame using glue and dowels, then glue in the tube dowels, tapping the tubes over the dowels and inserting flat bars into the slots.

9 Assemble the sides. Assemble the remaining side and base, inserting the tube dowel with glue added to the dowel holes. Position this side frame over the assembled frame and slot together, clamping until dry.

Two-hour, $25 bench

Need outdoor seating in a hurry? This simple bench, based on author and ecologist Aldo Leopold's classic design, can be constructed in a couple of hours. All it takes is two boards, some glue and 18 screws, for a cost of around $25.

Cut the legs from a 2x8 x 10-ft. piece of rot-resistant wood (Photo 1). Cut the seat and backrest from an 8-ft. 2x8.

Lay out and assemble the sides as mirror images, using the seat and back pieces for alignment (Photo 2). Join the legs with three 2-1/2-in. deck screws and construction adhesive. Predrill all the screw holes with a countersink bit to avoid splitting the wood.

Finally, set the sides up parallel to each other and glue and screw the seat and back into place. Finish the bench with a coat of exterior oil or stain.

Cutting list

Rear legs: 2x8 x 17-1/4" (22-1/2-degree cuts)
Front legs: 2x8 x 36" (22-1/2-degree cuts)
Seat: 2x8 x 42"
Back: 2x8 x 45"

1 Starting at one end of a 10-ft. board, make the same 22-1/2-degree cut five times to create the four legs.

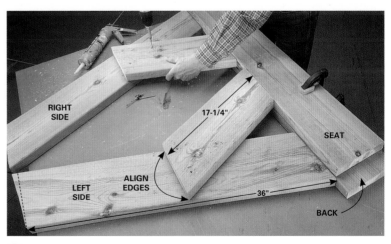

2 Clamp the seat and back to the workbench as a stop, then predrill, glue and screw the rear legs to the front legs.

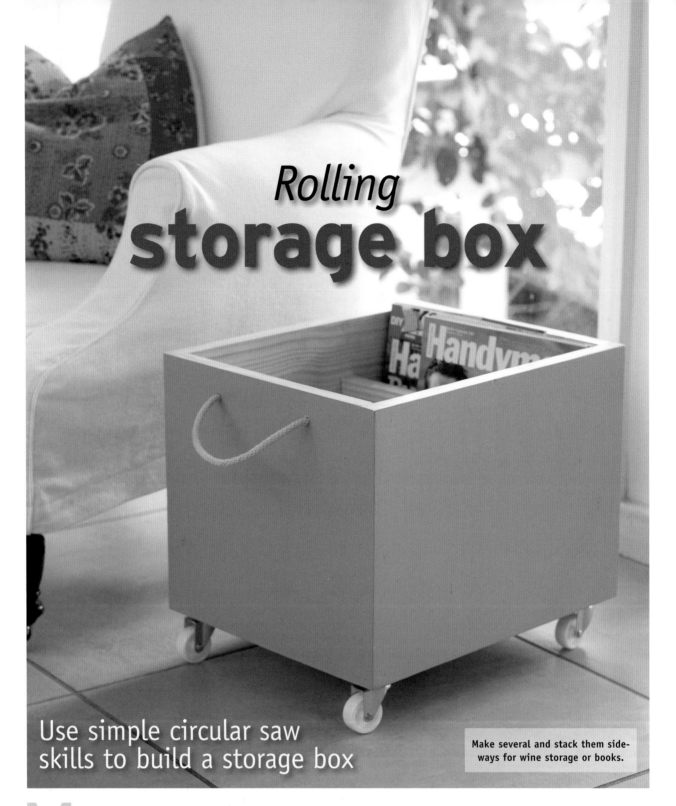

Rolling
storage box

Use simple circular saw skills to build a storage box

Make several and stack them sideways for wine storage or books.

Make a box from one 8-ft. length of 1x12 pine, a circular saw, a drill and a few hand tools.

The handles are made by drilling two 3/8-in. holes through the sides and feeding through 5/16-in. cotton sash rope. Tie the ends and add a drop of glue to prevent slipping. Add casters for mobility.

Cutting list

ITEM	QTY.	SIZE
Front and back	2	15-3/4" x 11-1/4" x 3/4"
Sides	2	11-1/4" x 11-1/4" x 3/4"
Base	1	14-1/4" x 11-1/4" x 3/4"
Dividers	2	11-1/4" x 8" x 3/4"

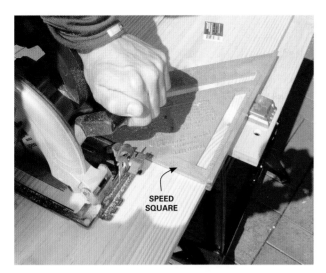

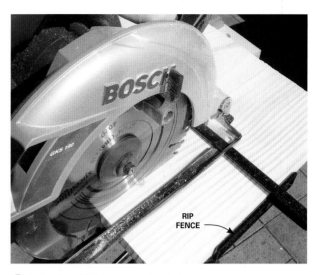

1 **Cut the pine.** Trim the ends of each board to make them square before marking and cutting to the required length (see the Cutting list). TIP: Use a Speed Square to guide the saw.

2 **Trim the dividers.** Set the rip fence on the saw to remove 3-1/4 in. from the sides of the dividers. Clamp the boards to cut them to the correct width. Check the sizes and label each piece. TIP: A 40- to 60-tooth blade cuts the pine cleanly.

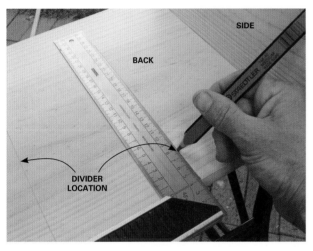

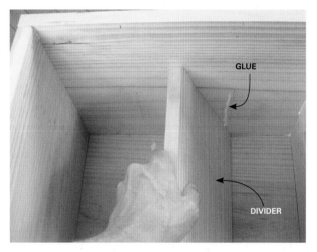

3 **Join the back and sides.** Join sides to the back, securing with glue and 6d finish nails (see Figure A). Mark the divider locations across the back.

4 **Attach the dividers.** Join the front and base to the frame with glue and nails. Apply glue on the divider layout lines, insert dividers, secure with glue and nails.

5 **Smooth the surfaces.** Drive the nail heads below the surface with a nail punch and fill with wood filler. When dry, sand all surfaces, joints and sharp edges using 180-grit sandpaper. Finish with a clear coat of varnish or two coats of interior paint. TIP: To prevent wood splitting at the edges, drill 3/32-in.-diameter holes for the nails before joining the panels.

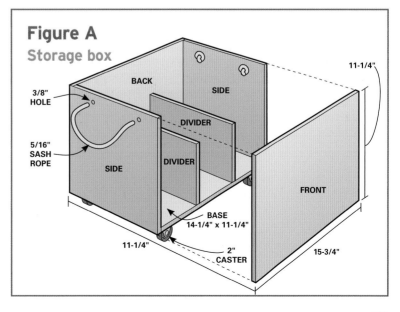

Figure A
Storage box

3/8" HOLE
5/16" SASH ROPE
BACK
SIDE
DIVIDER
DIVIDER
SIDE
FRONT
BASE 14-1/4" x 11-1/4"
2" CASTER
11-1/4"
11-1/4"
15-3/4"

Knock-apart table

This table is made from a full sheet of 5/8-in. plywood for the interlocking base stand and a sheet of 3/4-in. plywood for the work surface and shelves. You'll also need four 10-ft. lengths of 1x3 pine for the edge banding and cleats.

Cut two 30-in.-high by 48-in.-long pieces from the 5/8-in. plywood for the base pieces. Then cut a slightly oversize 5/8-in.-wide slot in the bottom half of one base and in the top half of the other. Make both slots about 15-1/2 in. long. Assemble the base and position the top so the corners are aligned with the legs. Screw loose-fitting 12-in.-long 1x3s along each side of each leg to hold everything stable.

The table is much more stable if you use the 3/4-in. waste from the top to make triangular braces (which also act as shelves) with 20-in.-long sides. Using 1-1/4-in. drywall screws, attach 1x2s to the base about 12 in. up from the floor and screw the shelves down.

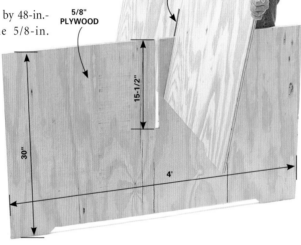

SLOT

5/8" PLYWOOD

15-1/2"

30"

4'

LOOSE FIT AGAINST LEG

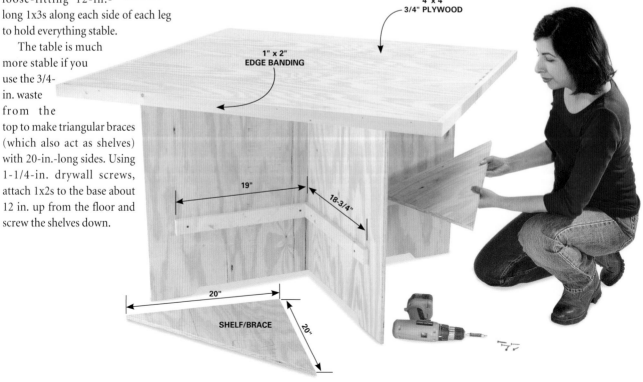

4' x 4' 3/4" PLYWOOD

1" x 2" EDGE BANDING

19"

18-3/4"

20"

20"

SHELF/BRACE

Light-duty table

If you ever need a light-duty work surface anywhere in the house for sewing, painting or school projects, this one's for you. Get to the home center and buy a hollow-core door; four toilet flanges; a 10-ft. length of 3-in. PVC pipe; 16 No. 10, 1-1/4-in.-long screws and a tube of construction adhesive. Inside of a half hour, you'll have the flanges glued and screwed to the door and be ready to slip in the 30-in.-long PVC legs.

CONSTRUCTION ADHESIVE

TOILET FLANGE

3" PVC PIPE

HOLLOW-CORE DOOR

30"

TOILET FLANGE

Three-hour
cedar bench
Build it in one afternoon!

The beauty of this cedar bench isn't just that it's easy to assemble and inexpensive—it's comfortable, too! The sloped back and seat are the secrets to pain-free perching on unpadded flat boards. (Of course, you could add cushions if you'd like.) This bench has a bolted pivot point where the back and seat meet that lets you alter the backrest and seat slopes to fit your build during one of the final assembly steps (Photo 10). Cutting and assembly will only take about three hours. Follow the step-by-step photo series for details on the simple construction.

Build it from eight 8-ft.-long boards

A circular saw and a screw gun are the only power tools you really need for construction, although a power miter saw will speed things up and give you cleaner cuts. Begin by cutting the boards to length. Figure A shows you how to cut the eight boards efficiently, leaving little waste.

After cutting the pieces to length, screw together the leg assemblies (Photos 2 – 6). Be sure to use a square to keep the leg braces square to the legs (Photo 2). That way both leg assemblies will be identical and the bench won't wobble if it's put on a hard,

Figure A
Bench parts

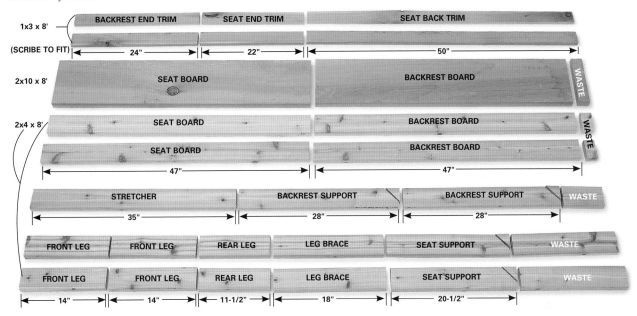

1x3 x 8'	BACKREST END TRIM	SEAT END TRIM	SEAT BACK TRIM
(SCRIBE TO FIT)	24"	22"	50"

2x10 x 8'
SEAT BOARD — BACKREST BOARD — WASTE

2x4 x 8'
SEAT BOARD — BACKREST BOARD — WASTE
SEAT BOARD — BACKREST BOARD
47" — 47"

STRETCHER — BACKREST SUPPORT — BACKREST SUPPORT — WASTE
35" — 28" — 28"

FRONT LEG — FRONT LEG — REAR LEG — LEG BRACE — SEAT SUPPORT — WASTE
FRONT LEG — FRONT LEG — REAR LEG — LEG BRACE — SEAT SUPPORT — WASTE
14" — 14" — 11-1/2" — 18" — 20-1/2"

1 Cut out the bench parts following the measurements in Figure A. Use a Speed Square to guide the circular saw for accurate, square cuts. Cut 45-degree angles on the ends of the seat and back supports 1 in. down from the ends as shown (also see Photos 4 and 5).

SPEED SQUARE

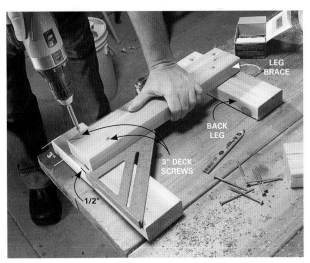

LEG BRACE

BACK LEG

3" DECK SCREWS

3"

1/2"

2 Fasten the leg brace to the legs 3 in. above the bottom ends. Angle the 3-in. screws slightly to prevent the screw tips from protruding through the other side. Hold the brace 1/2 in. back from the front edge of the front leg. Use a square to make sure the brace and legs are at exact right angles.

flat surface. The leg brace is spaced 1/2 in. back from the front of the legs to create a more attractive shadow line. Then it's just a matter of connecting the leg assemblies with the stretcher (Photo 7), screwing down the seat and backrest boards and adjusting the slopes to fit your body.

The easiest way to adjust the slope is to hold the four locking points in place with clamps and then back out the temporary screws (Photo 10). To customize the slopes, you just loosen the clamps, make the adjustments, retighten and test the fit. When you're satisfied, run a couple of permanent screws into each joint. If you don't have clamps, don't worry—you'll just have to back out the screws, adjust the slopes, reset the screws and test the bench. Clamps just speed up the process.

Materials list

ITEM	QTY.	ITEM	QTY.
1x3 x 8' cedar	2	6d galv. casing nails	1/4 lb.
2x10 x 8' cedar	1		
2x4 x 8' cedar	5	3/8" x 5" bolts with nuts and washers	2
3" deck screws	1 lb.		

Round over the edges

Photo 12 shows rounding over the sharp edge of the 1x3 trim, which is best done with a router and a 1/2-in. round-over bit.

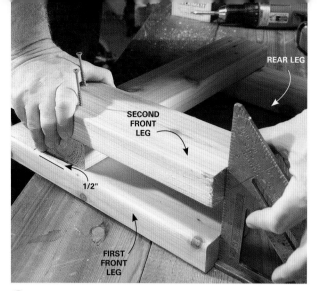

3 Align the second part of the front leg with the first one using a square and screw it to the leg brace as shown.

Labels on image: REAR LEG, SECOND FRONT LEG, 1/2", FIRST FRONT LEG

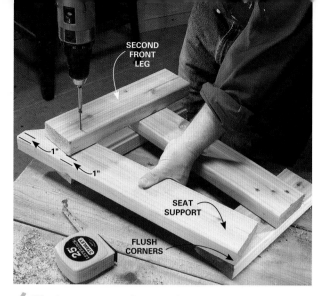

4 Slip the seat support between the two front legs, positioning it as shown. Drive a single 3-in. screw through the front leg into the seat support.

Labels on image: SECOND FRONT LEG, 1", 1", SEAT SUPPORT, FLUSH CORNERS

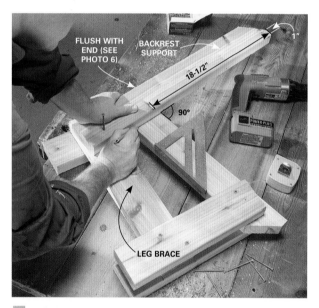

5 Position the backrest support on the leg assembly as shown, making sure it's at a right angle with the seat support, and mark the position on the seat support. Then drive a 3-in. screw through the middle of the backrest support into the leg brace.

Labels on image: FLUSH WITH END (SEE PHOTO 6), BACKREST SUPPORT, 1", 18-1/2", 90°, LEG BRACE

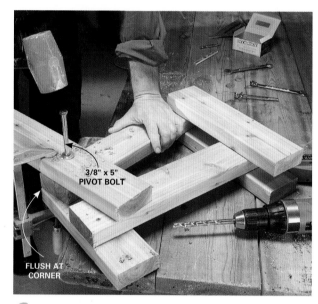

6 Clamp the backrest support, seat support and rear leg as shown using the line as a guide. Drill a 3/8-in. hole through the center of the assembly. Drive a 3/8-in. x 5-in. bolt fitted with a washer through the hole and slightly tighten the nut against a washer on the other side.

Labels on image: 3/8" x 5" PIVOT BOLT, FLUSH AT CORNER

Rounding over the edges can protect shins and the backs of thighs and leave teetering toddlers with goose eggs on their melons instead of gashes. So the step is highly recommended. If you don't have a router, round over the edge either by hand-sanding or with an orbital or belt sander. In any event, keep the casing nails 1 in. away from the edge to prevent hitting the nail heads with the router bit or sandpaper (Photo 12).

Building a longer bench

Shown is a 4-ft. long bench, with plenty of space for two. But you can use the same design and techniques for building 6- or 8-ft.-long benches too. You'll just have to buy longer boards for the seat, back, stretcher and the trim boards. While you're at it, you can use the same design for matching end or coffee tables. Just match the double front leg design for the rear legs, and build flat-topped leg assemblies with an overall depth of 16-3/4 in.

Seal the legs to make it last

If you want to stain your bench, use a latex exterior stain on the parts after cutting them to length. After assembly, you won't be able to get good penetration at the cracks and crevices. Avoid clear exterior sealers, which will irritate bare skin. But the bench will last outside for more than 20 years without any stain or special care even if you decide to let it weather to a natural gray. However, the legs won't last that long, because the end grain at the bottom will wick up moisture from the ground, making the legs rot long before the bench does. To make sure the legs last as long as the bench, seal the ends with epoxy, urethane or exterior woodworker's glue when you're through with the assembly.

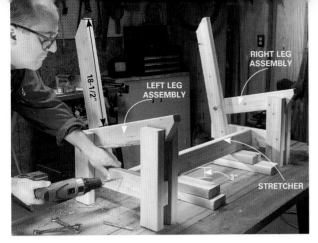

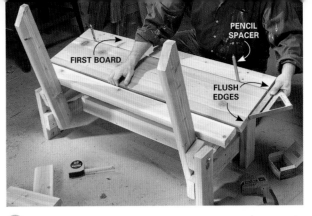

7 Assemble the other leg assembly to mirror the first as shown. (The back support and rear leg switch sides.) Prop the stretcher 3 in. above the workbench, center it between the front and rear bench legs and screw the leg braces into the ends with two 3-in. deck screws.

8 Center the first 2x4 seat board over the leg assemblies and flush with the front ends of the seat supports. Screw it to the seat supports with two 3-in. deck screws spaced about 1 in. away from the edges. Line up the 2x10 with the first 2x4, space it about 5/16 in. away (the thickness of a carpenter's pencil) and screw it to the seat supports with two 3-in. deck screws. Repeat with the rear 2x4.

9 Rest the bottom backrest 2x4 on carpenter's pencils, holding the end flush with the seat boards and screw it to the seat back braces. Then space and screw on the center 2x10 and the top 2x4 backrest boards.

10 Sit on the bench and decide if you'd like to tilt the seat or the backrest or both to make the bench more comfortable. To make seat or back adjustments, loosen the bolts and clamp the bottoms of the seat back supports and the fronts of the seat supports. Then back out the four screws at those points. Loosen the clamps, make adjustments, then retighten and retest for comfort. When you're satisfied with the fit, drive in the four original screws plus another at each point. Retighten the pivot bolts.

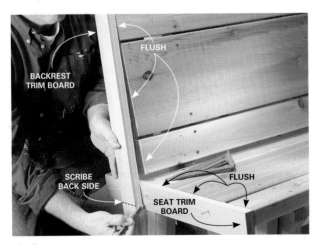

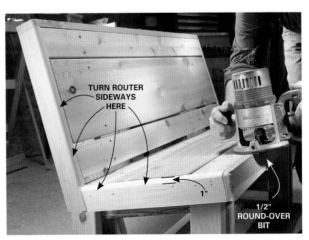

11 Tack the seat trim boards to the seat with the ends flush with the front and top. Scribe and cut the trim boards to fit. Nail the boards to the seat and backrest boards with 6d galvanized casing nails. Keep the nails 1 in. from the seat edges.

12 Ease the edges of the trim boards with a router and a 1/2-in. round-over bit. Hold the router sideways to get at the seat/back corner.

Stone-top table

The inspiration for this small end table came while browsing through a local tile store, looking at the huge variety of slate, granite, limestone and marble that's now available. The table top shown here is 16-in.-square copper slate—a perfect match for the oak base—but many other stone tiles are available.

To make this table, you'll need a power miter saw, drill and hand tools. The stone top doesn't need cutting—just soften the sharp edges with 120-grit sandpaper. The base is made from standard dimension oak, available at home centers. And once you put together the simple cutting and assembly jigs shown in the photos on the next page, the table base almost builds itself.

Figure A
Stone-top table

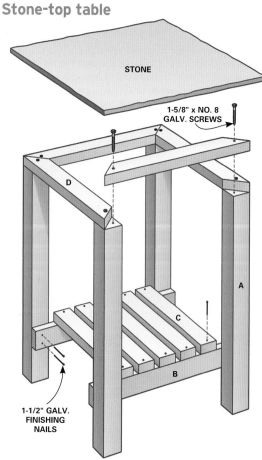

STONE

1-5/8" x NO. 8 GALV. SCREWS

D

A

C

B

1-1/2" GALV. FINISHING NAILS

Materials list

Wood

2	2x2 x 3' oak
14'	1x2 oak

Stone Tile

1	16" x 16" x 1/2"

Hardware

1 lb.	1-1/2" galvanized finishing nails
8	1-5/8" x No. 8 galvanized screws
4	Nylon chair glides
	Exterior wood glue
	Exterior construction adhesive

BLACK SLATE

CREAM QUARTZ

INDIAN AUTUMN SLATE

Cutting list

KEY	NAME	QTY.	DIMENSIONS
A	Leg	4	2x2 x 16-3/4"
B	Shelf supports	2	1x2 x 13-3/4"
C	Shelf slats	5	1x2 x 10-3/4"
D	Mitered top support	4	1x2 x 13-3/4"

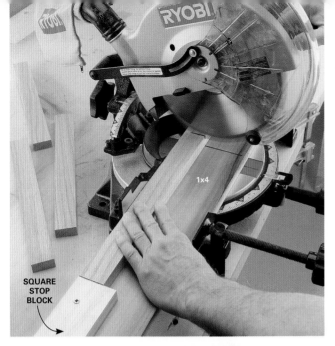

MITERED STOP BLOCK

SQUARE STOP BLOCK

1x4

1 Make a jig with square and mitered stop blocks screwed to a straight 1x4. Slide the 1x4 to the right length for each piece and clamp it down. When you cut the miters, set the saw for 45-1/2 degrees. That way, the outside corners of the top—the only part that shows—will be tight even if the top isn't perfectly square. Sand all the oak pieces before beginning assembly.

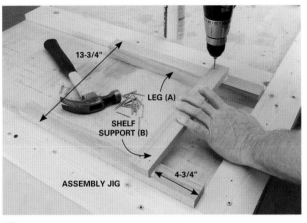

13-3/4"

LEG (A)

SHELF SUPPORT (B)

4-3/4"

ASSEMBLY JIG

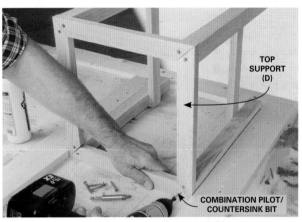

TOP SUPPORT (D)

COMBINATION PILOT/ COUNTERSINK BIT

2 Set up a square assembly jig with 1x4s attached to your workbench. Use two shelf supports as spacers to ensure that the jig is the correct width. Set two table legs (A) in the jig and attach a shelf support (B) with glue and nails. Predrill with a 5/64-in. drill bit, or use one of the nails with the head clipped off as the drill bit.

3 Screw down the mitered top supports (D) with the table still in the jig, using glue and 1-5/8-in. galvanized screws. Predrill and countersink with a combination bit at a slight angle, toward the center of the leg.

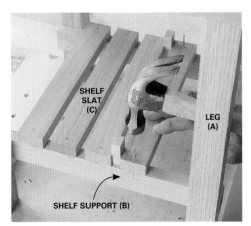

SHELF SLAT (C)

LEG (A)

SHELF SUPPORT (B)

CONSTRUCTION ADHESIVE

5 Glue the stone top to the base. First, center the table and trace the top onto the tile. Lay a bead of construction adhesive within the outline, keeping the glue away from the outer edge to avoid oozing. Press the table into the glue. Place a weight on the table for 24 hours until the glue sets. Leave excess glue until it's dry, and then peel it away. Finish the wood with exterior oil or varnish and add a nylon chair glide on the bottom of each leg.

4 Predrill and nail the shelf slats with the legs tight and square against the sides of the assembly jig. Attach the center slat first, centering it on the shelf support. Wipe off excess glue and set the remaining slats, using two 1/2-in. spacers. Set the nails, fill the holes, then sand.

Sturdy, stable stool

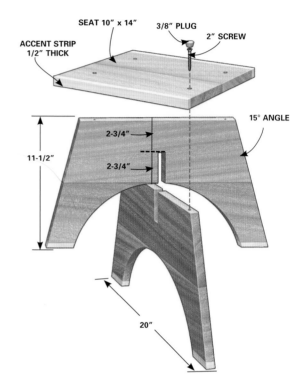

SEAT 10" x 14"

3/8" PLUG

2" SCREW

ACCENT STRIP
1/2" THICK

15° ANGLE

2-3/4"

11-1/2"

2-3/4"

20"

This stool is as practical as it is beautiful. The crossed, flared legs make it stable, strong and quick to build. Start by gluing 4-1/2-in.-wide boards together (Photo 1) for the seat and 5-1/2-in.-wide boards for the legs. Rip 1/2-in.-wide contrasting accent strips on a table saw and glue them into place.

Next, mark the leg blanks, beginning with a center line (Photo 2). To mark the angled end cuts, measure 10 in. from the center line at the bottom and then draw a 15-degree angle. Make a trammel to mark the arcs: Drill a pencil hole in a strip of wood, then drive a screw 8 in. from the center of the pencil hole. Cut the arc with a jigsaw and sand it smooth. If the table saw is large enough, use it to cut the angled ends of the legs. Otherwise, use a circular saw and sand the cut smooth.

Cut the notches in the legs with a small pull saw (Photo 3). With both sides of the notch cut, break out the middle and smooth the bottom of the notch with a chisel. Slip the two legs together. If light hammer taps won't drive the legs together, hone down the tight spots with a file.

With the seat lying upside down, set the leg assembly on it and trace the outline of the legs. Drill marker holes through the seat from the underside at each of the four screw locations using a 1/16-in. bit. Then flip the top over and drill a 3/8-in. hole 3/8 in. deep at each marker hole. Use a brad-point bit for these holes to avoid splintering. Set the seat on the legs, drill 1/8-in. pilot holes and screw the seat to the legs.

Materials: 10 ft. of walnut 1x6, 2 ft. of maple 1x2, wood glue, 2-in. screws, 3/8-in. maple plugs, spray lacquer.

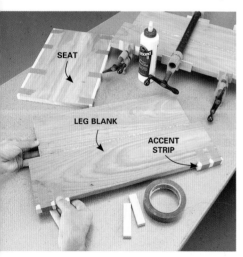

1 Glue and clamp boards together to form the top and legs. Add accent strips, using masking tape to hold the strips until the glue dries.

SEAT

LEG BLANK

ACCENT STRIP

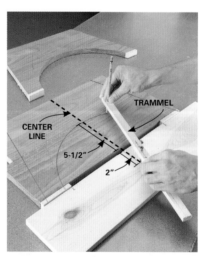

2 Mark the arcs with a homemade trammel. Draw center lines on the legs to accurately position the arcs, the end cuts and the notches you'll cut next.

TRAMMEL

CENTER LINE

5-1/2"

2"

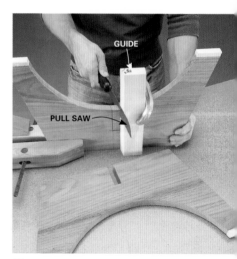

3 Cut perfect notches using a guide block to steer your saw. To make the guide, cut a scrap of wood on a table saw with the blade set to 15 degrees.

GUIDE

PULL SAW

Bonus section:

Paint Anything Guide

DIYers know that if you want big impact FAST—paint! You can completely change the look and feel of a room with freshly painted walls, trim or both. For the cost of paint and supplies, you can transform a room in just one day.

Here are a few of our best quick painting tips, followed by 21 pages of expert how-to advice to help you achieve a professional-looking paint job, even if it's your first try.

Paint all four sides of spindles at once

Finishing spindles is a pain because you have to finish three sides, let them dry and then turn them over and do the unfinished side. But not if you drive long drywall screws into the spindle ends and then rest the screws on two boards or sawhorses. An added bonus is that you can keep your fingers out of the wet finish by holding onto the screws as you paint and turn.

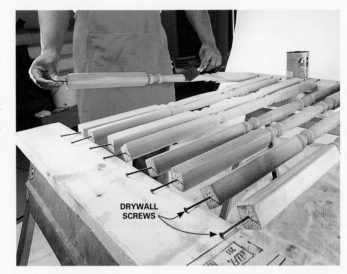

DRYWALL SCREWS

Scrape away ceiling texture

A neat, straight paint line at the top of a wall is tough to achieve next to a bumpy ceiling. So before you paint, drag a narrow flathead screwdriver lightly along the ceiling to knock off the texture. You'll get a clean paint line and no one will ever notice that the texture is missing.

Self-stick paint shield

Glad Press 'n Seal plastic wrap (at discount stores and supermarkets) goes on fast and stays right where you put it. Paint can seep under the edges, though, so it's no substitute for masking tape in spots where you need a crisp edge.

Trim painting tips

Repainting chipped, flaking, dirty moldings can transform a room. But for a crisp, professional-looking job, you have to go beyond just brushing on a coat of paint. From prep work to the final coat, here are tips for making your painted woodwork look like new.

NO-LOAD SANDPAPER

Careful sanding is the key to a perfect job

If your woodwork is smooth, just give it a once-over with 120-grit sandpaper. But if your trim is in rough shape like the trim shown here, start with 80-grit sandpaper. Switch to 100-grit for smoothing and blending in the areas with layered paint. Finally, go over all the wood with 120-grit. Buy sandpaper labeled "no-load." No-load sandpaper won't clog as easily and is better for sanding painted surfaces.

SPACKLING COMPOUND

Fill holes and dents

To repair large dents or gouges on edges that are vulnerable to abuse, use hardening-type two-part wood filler (Minwax High Performance Wood Filler is one brand). Fill smaller dents and holes with spackling compound. Since spackling compound shrinks as it dries, you'll have to apply a second (and possibly a third) coat after the previous coat dries.

Shine a strong light across the woodwork to highlight depressions and ensure that you don't miss any spots as you're applying the filler. Let the filler dry and sand it smooth.

CAULKED CRACK

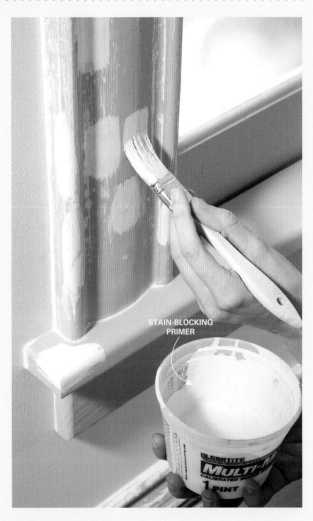

STAIN-BLOCKING PRIMER

Caulk for a seamless look

Here's a step that many beginners don't know about but pros swear by. Caulk every crack or gap, no matter how small. Use latex caulk or a paintable latex/silicone blend. The key is to cut the caulk tube tip very carefully to create a tiny, 1/16-in.-diameter hole. Fill all the small cracks first. Then, if you have wider cracks to fill, recut the caulk tube tip to make a larger hole. Move the caulk gun swiftly along the cracks to avoid an excess buildup of caulk. If necessary, smooth the caulk with your fingertip. Keep a damp rag in your pocket to clean caulk from your finger and to keep the tip of the caulk tube clean. If caulk piles up in the corners, remove the excess with a flexible putty knife.

Spot-prime to avoid blotches

Brush a stain-sealing primer (BIN is one brand of shellac-based primer) over the areas that you've patched or filled, and over areas where you've sanded down to bare wood. If you have a lot of patches and bare spots, it'll be faster and easier to just prime the entire surface. Also seal discolored areas or marks left by crayons, pens or markers to prevent them from bleeding through the finish coat of paint.

Add an extender to latex paint

Most pros prefer to use oil-based paint on trim for two reasons: Oil-based paint doesn't dry as fast as water-based paint, leaving more time to brush. And oil-based paint levels out better than most water-based paints, leaving a smoother surface with few visible brush marks. But because water-based paint is more environmentally friendly, less stinky and easier to clean up, it's a better choice for DIYers.

You can make water-based paint perform more like oil paint by adding latex paint conditioner. Floetrol is one brand. Conditioners, also called extenders, make the paint flow better and slow down the drying time, allowing you more time to spread the paint without leaving brush marks. Check with the manufacturer of the paint you're using to see if it recommends a particular brand of conditioner.

LATEX PAINT CONDITIONER

Paint from a separate pail

Pour paint about 1-1/2-in.-deep into a separate pail. A metal painter's pail (shown below); a specialty pail called a Handy Paint Pail (handypaintpail.com, at paint stores and home centers); and even an empty 5-quart ice cream pail all work great. Placing a small amount of paint in a pail allows you to easily load the bristles of the brush by dipping them about 1 in. into the paint.

Slap, don't wipe

Slap the brush gently against each side of the bucket to remove the excess paint. This method of brush loading is best for laying on paint because it keeps the bristles fully loaded with paint. To use the brush for cutting-in, follow up by wiping each side of the brush gently on the rim to remove a little more paint.

CUT-IN LINE

Cut in edges before you fill the center

Cutting-in is a skill that takes practice to master, but it's worth the effort. To cut in, first load the brush. Then wipe most of the excess paint off by gently scraping the bristles on the edge of the can. Start by pulling the brush along the edge, but keep the bristles about 1/4 in. away from the wall or ceiling to deposit some paint on the wood. Now return with another brushstroke, this time a little closer. Sneaking up to the line like this is easier than trying to get it perfect on the first try. At the end of the stroke, arc the brush away from the cut-in line. Cut in a few feet and then fill the middle using the lay-on, lay-off technique we show in the next section.

LAYING-OFF STROKE

BRUSH MARK

Lay on, lay off

The biggest mistake beginners make is to work the paint too long after it's applied. Remember, the paint starts to dry as soon as you put it on, and you have to smooth it out before this happens or you'll end up with brushstrokes or worse. So here's the tip. Load your brush. Then quickly unload on the surface with a few back-and-forth brushstrokes. This is called "laying on" the paint. Repeat this until you've covered a few feet of trim with paint. Don't worry about how it looks yet.

Now, without reloading the brush, drag the tips of the bristles over the wet paint in one long stroke to "lay off" the paint. Start in the unpainted area and drag into the previously painted trim. Sweep your brush up off the surface at the end of each stroke. Areas wider than your brush will require several parallel laying-off strokes to finish. When you're done laying off a section, move on and repeat the process, always working quickly to avoid brushing over partially dried paint. Try to complete shorter pieces of trim with a continuous laying-off brushstroke.

Don't start a brushstroke on already-smoothed paint

Setting the paintbrush on an area that's already been smoothed out with laying-off strokes will leave an unsightly mark. Try to start laying-off strokes at the end of a trim piece or board, or in an unpainted area. Brush toward the finished area. Then sweep the brush up and off, like an airplane taking off from a runway, to avoid leaving a mark.

Don't brush across an edge

Brushing across an edge wipes paint from the bristles and creates a heavy buildup of paint that will run or drip. Avoid this by brushing toward edges whenever possible. If you must start a brushstroke at an edge, align the bristles carefully as if you're cutting-in, instead of wiping them against the edge. If you accidentally get a buildup of paint that could cause a run, spread it out right away with a dry paintbrush or wipe it off with a damp rag or your finger.

DON'T

Prep problem walls for painting

It doesn't matter how much abuse your walls have taken; you can repair them and make them perfectly smooth. Most repairs are inexpensive and take only a few hours. If you hired a pro to do the work, you'd pay hundreds of dollars. That's because the pro would have to make many trips to your house to complete the job (most fixes require two or three coats of joint compound).

Here you'll learn how to fix common wall problems before you paint. Everything you need is available at home centers. For small fixes, pick up spackling compound. For larger repairs, use all-purpose joint compound. You may also need mesh tape.

Highlight hidden flaws

Minor wall flaws are often hard to spot—until the afternoon sun hits them and makes them embarrassingly obvious. Find and mark any imperfections in the walls. Start by turning off all the lights in the room and closing the curtains. Then hold a trouble light next to the wall and move it across the surface (a process called "raking").

Wherever the light highlights a problem, even a small one, stick a piece of tape next to it so you can easily find it when you come through with spackling or joint compound. Tape works better than circling the problems with a pencil or pen (which can bleed through the paint).

MARK FLAW WITH TAPE

FLAW

Highlight hard-to-see flaws with a strong light. The shadows cast by small bumps and dents are easy to spot.

Fix nail pops forever

Seasonal expansion and contraction of studs can push nails out of the drywall. You can't just resink the nail and apply joint compound over the top—the nail will pop back out. To permanently fix the problem, drive a drywall screw about 2 in. above or below the popped nail. Use a 1-1/4-in. screw (screws hold better than nails). A longer screw isn't better—it's actually more likely to pop out than a shorter one.

Now pull out the nail, holding a wide putty knife under your pry bar to protect the wall. Tap the empty nail hole with the putty knife handle to knock protruding drywall fragments into the wall (or you won't get a smooth coat of filler on the wall). Finally, cover the screw head and fill the nail hole with three coats of joint compound.

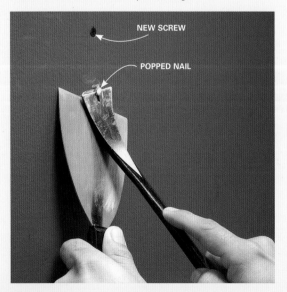

NEW SCREW

POPPED NAIL

Seal torn paper

The back of a chair, a flying video game remote or an aggressive kid with a toy truck can tear the drywall paper face. A coat of paint or joint compound over torn paper will create a fuzzy texture. For a smooth finish, seal the torn paper. Start by cutting away any loose paper. Then seal the exposed drywall with a stain-blocking primer. This keeps the drywall from absorbing moisture from the soon-to-be-applied joint compound. Wait for the primer to dry, then sand the exposed drywall edges to remove paper nubs. Cover the gouge with a thin layer of joint compound, feathering it out along the wall. If necessary, apply a second coat, feathering it as well, then wait for it to dry and sand it smooth.

PRIMER

tip After applying joint compound, be sure to cover it with primer before painting to prevent "flashing." Flashing occurs when joint compound absorbs the paint, dulling the finish.

Tape and fill damaged corners

Metal corner bead dents easily, causing cracks in the wall. Fortunately, the fix is relatively simple too. Use a hammer to knock the bead back into shape with several light taps instead of hard blows (Photo 1). Use a level to make sure the bead doesn't stick out past the finished walls or you won't get a clean corner (bury the bead in the wall a little if needed). Round any sharp edges on the bead with a file.

When you hit the bead with a hammer, you probably sent cracks up and down the corner, especially if the bead wasn't taped. Place mesh tape over the cracks, then apply joint compound over the tape and corner bead on one side only (Photo 2). Work on one side at a time—the first side needs to be hard so you can square the other side. Once the first side is dry, apply joint compound to the second side. Then recoat the corner, let it dry and sand it smooth.

1 Shape the corner bead with a hammer until it's flush with the walls. Don't worry about making drywall cracks along the corner worse.

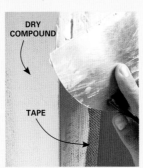

DRY COMPOUND

TAPE

2 Cover the crack with mesh tape, then cover the tape and the corner bead with joint compound. Fill in one side, let it dry, then fill in the other side.

Cut around glue spots

Mirrors and paneling are sometimes installed with an adhesive backing to help hold them in place. But when you take them down, the glue sticks to the drywall. Don't try to pull it off—you'll tear the drywall face, making rips across the wall. Instead, cut around the glue with a utility knife, cutting through the drywall face.

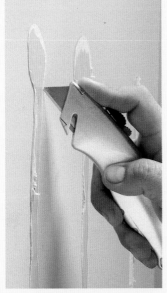

Scrape off the glue with a putty knife. You'll still tear the paper, but the tears will be confined to the outline you cut in the drywall. Use sandpaper on small areas of glue that won't scrape off. Fill gouges that you made in the wall with joint compound (see "Seal Torn Paper," p. 128).

Fill holes three times

Fill small holes and indents (less than 1/8 in.) with spackling compound. For larger holes, use joint compound instead.

Apply either compound with a putty knife, spreading it thin on the wall. You'll apply two more coats (the compounds shrink as they dry), so don't worry if the hole isn't filled perfectly the first time. Let each coat of compound dry (read the directions; some dry in just two hours).

Don't believe spackling labels that say you don't have to sand—you do. You'll have to sand between coats if there's any excess compound. After the final coat, use fine-grit paper.

Cut out wall cracks

When homes settle, drywall cracks sometimes shoot out above or below windows and above doors. You can't just cover or fill the cracks with joint compound—they'll come back. Instead, fix the cracks with joint compound and mesh tape. Mesh tape gives you less buildup than paper tape and is plenty strong. Protect the window or door trim with masking tape before starting the fix.

To fill the crack, use a utility knife to cut a V-shaped groove along its entire length (Photo 1). Fill the groove with joint compound, let it dry, then sand it flush with the wall. Place mesh tape over the crack (Photo 2). Apply joint compound over the tape and feather it out 2 to 4 in. on each side of the tape. Let the compound dry, then apply a second and third coat, feathering it out 8 to 10 in. from the tape with a 10-in. taping blade.

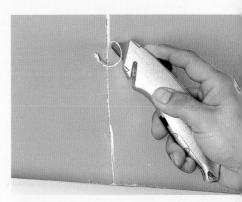

1 Cut a V-shaped groove in the crack, removing everything that's loose, even if it means cutting all the way through to the back of the drywall.

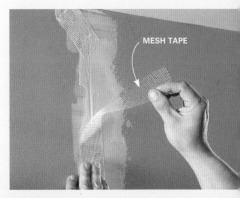

MESH TAPE

2 Fill the groove with joint compound, cover it with mesh tape, then cover it with more compound.

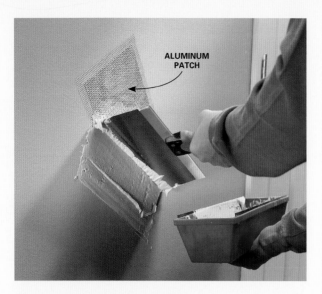

ALUMINUM PATCH

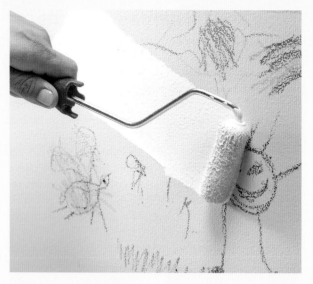

Fix holes fast with an aluminum patch

The old method of repairing large holes was to cut out a square in the drywall, attach wood backing and then screw on a new patch of drywall. Aluminum patches are a faster, easier solution. Cut the patch so it covers the hole by at least 1 in. on each side, then place it over the hole. One side is sticky to adhere to the wall. Cover the patch with joint compound. Let it dry overnight, then recoat.

Block stains with special primer

Don't expect regular primer or paint to cover marker or crayon marks; they'll bleed through even several coats of paint. The same goes for water stains. First try to wash off the marker or crayon with a Mr. Clean Magic Eraser dipped in warm water. If that doesn't work, cover the marks with stain-blocking primer (KILZ and BIN are two brands). Apply the primer with a roller so the texture will match the rest of the wall. Buy a cheap disposable roller and then throw it away when you're done.

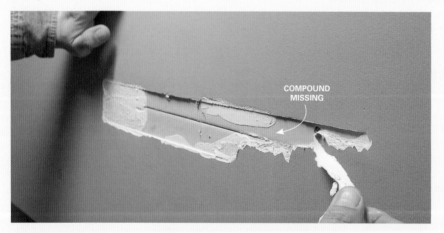

COMPOUND MISSING

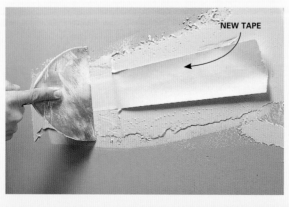

NEW TAPE

1 Cut away loose tape with a utility knife. Be aggressive and cut past where the tape has lifted away from the wall.

2 Place a strip of tape in joint compound a few inches past and directly over the patch. Apply joint compound over the top of the tape.

Replace lifting tape

Tape will lift off the wall if there isn't enough joint compound underneath to adhere it to the drywall. You'll have to cut away the loose tape and replace it. Start by cutting through the paint and joint compound to remove every piece of loose tape. Go beyond the cracked area. Peel away the tape until you see the underlying drywall (Photo 1). Then fill the hole with joint compound and wait for it to harden. Embed mesh or paper tape in joint compound over the hole (Photo 2). Extend the tape a few inches past the hole on each side. Once it's dry, apply a second coat and feather it to blend the patch with the wall.

Rolling techniques

Most people have used paint rollers before, with varying degrees of success. Maybe they just plunged right in and started rolling, developing their own technique as they went. Or maybe they read the instructions telling them to apply the paint in some pattern, usually a "W," before rolling it out. Here you'll learn a slightly different approach: how to simply and quickly spread a smooth, even coat of latex paint on the wall. It's not fancy, but it gets the job done in record time and eliminates common problems like light areas, roller marks and built-up ridges that sometimes plague first-time painters.

However, even the best technique won't work with poor-quality equipment. Don't waste your money on those all-in-one throwaway roller setups when you can buy a pro setup that will last a lifetime. Start with a good roller frame. Buy one that is sturdy and is designed to keep the roller cover from slipping off while you paint (see photo, right).

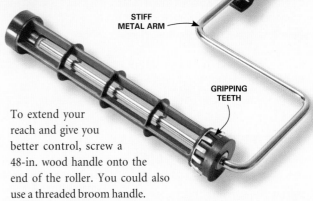

STIFF METAL ARM

GRIPPING TEETH

To extend your reach and give you better control, screw a 48-in. wood handle onto the end of the roller. You could also use a threaded broom handle.

You'll need a container for the paint. While most homeowners use paint trays, you'll rarely see a pro using one. That's because a 5-gallon bucket with a special bucket screen hung over the edge works a lot better.

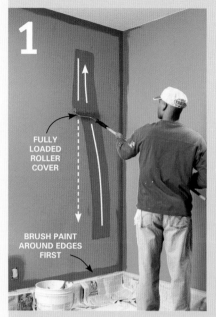

(1) Lay the paint on the wall with a sweeping stroke. Start about a foot from the bottom and 6 in. from the corner and roll upward at a slight angle using light pressure. Stop a few inches from the ceiling. Now roll up and down, back toward the corner to quickly spread the paint. You can leave paint buildup and roller marks at this step. Don't worry about a perfect job yet. **(2)** Reload the roller and repeat the process in the adjacent space, working back toward the painted area.

(3) Roll back over the entire area you've covered to smooth and blend the paint. Don't reload the roller with paint for this step. Use very light pressure. Roll up and down, from floor to ceiling and move over about three-quarters of a roller width each time so you're always slightly overlapping the previous stroke. When you reach the corner, roll as close as you can to the adjacent wall without touching it. Repeat Steps 1 through 3 until the entire wall is painted.

Here are a few of the advantages of a bucket and screen over a roller pan:

- It's easy to move the bucket without spilling.
- The bucket holds more paint. You won't have to frequently refill a pan.
- You're less likely to trip over or step in a bucket of paint.
- It's quicker and easier to load the roller cover with paint from a bucket.
- It's easy to cover a bucket with a damp cloth to prevent the paint from drying out while you're taking a lunch break.

Use an old drywall compound bucket or buy a clean new bucket. Add a bucket screen and you're ready to go.

Take a wool-blend roller cover for a spin

The most important part of your paint rolling setup is the roller cover, also known as a sleeve. It's tempting to buy the cheapest cover available and throw it away when you're done. But you won't mind the few extra minutes of cleanup time once you experience the difference a

Load the roller cover by dipping into the paint about 1/2 in. and then rolling it against the screen. Filling a dry roller cover with paint will require five or six repetitions. After that, two or three dips are all you need. Leave the roller almost dripping with paint.

good roller cover makes. Cheap roller covers don't hold enough paint to do a good job. It'll take you four times as long to paint a room. And you'll likely end up with an inconsistent layer of paint, lap marks and built-up ridges of paint.

Instead, buy a 1/2-in. nap, wool-blend roller cover and give it a try. (One good one is a combination of polyester for ease of use and wool for maximum paint capacity.) With proper care, this may be the last roller cover you'll ever buy.

Wool covers do have a few drawbacks, though. They tend to shed fibers when they're first used. To minimize shedding, wrap the new roller cover with masking tape and peel it off to remove loose fibers. Repeat this a few times. Wool covers also tend to become matted down if you apply too much pressure while painting. Rolling demands a light touch. No matter what roller cover you're using, always let the paint do the work. Keep the roller cover loaded with paint and use only enough pressure to release and spread the paint. Pushing on the roller to squeeze out the last drop of paint will only cause problems.

The best coat of paint can't hide bumpy walls

Fill holes with lightweight spackling compound and sand them smooth when it dries. Then go over the entire wall with 100-grit sandpaper mounted in a drywall sanding handle. The ultimate setup for this job is a pole-mounted drywall sander with a 100-grit mesh drywall sanding screen, but any method of sanding off old paint lumps and bumps will do. Next mask off the baseboard and window and door trim. Slide the blade of a flexible putty knife along the edge of the masking tape to seal it. Otherwise paint will bleed underneath.

Tips for a perfect paint job

■ Keep a wet edge. Keeping a wet edge is crucial to all top-quality finish jobs, whether you're enameling a door, finishing furniture or rolling paint on a wall. The idea is to plan the sequence of work and work fast enough so that you're always lapping newly applied paint onto paint that's still wet. If you stop for a break in the middle of a wall, for example, and then start painting after this section has dried, you'll likely see a lap mark where the two areas join. The rolling technique shown in the sequence on p. 132 avoids this problem by allowing you to quickly cover a large area with paint and then return to smooth it out.

■ Lay it on, smooth it off. The biggest mistake most beginning painters make, whether they're brushing or rolling, is taking too long to apply the paint. Photo 1 on p. 132 shows how to lay on the paint. Then quickly spread it out and repeat the laying-on process again (Photo 2). This will only work with a good-quality roller cover that holds a lot of paint. Until you're comfortable with the technique and get a feel for how quickly the paint is drying, cover only about 3 or 4 ft. of wall before smoothing off the whole area (Photo 3). If you find the paint is drying slowly, you can cover an entire wall before smoothing it off.

4 Smooth the paint along the ceiling using a long horizontal stroke without reloading the roller with paint.

■ Get as close as you can. Since rollers can't get tight to edges, the first painting step is to brush along the ceiling, inside corners and moldings. This "cutting in" process leaves brush marks that won't match the roller texture on the rest of the wall. For the best-looking job, you'll want to cover as many brush marks as possible with the roller. Do this by carefully rolling up close to inside corners, moldings and the ceiling. Face the open end of the roller toward the edge and remember not to use a roller that's fully loaded with paint. With practice, you'll be able to get within an inch of the ceiling rolling vertically, and can avoid crawling up on a ladder to paint horizontally, as shown in Photo 4.

Avoid fat edges and roller marks

Ridges of paint left by the edge of the roller, called "fat edges," are a common problem. And if left to dry, they can be difficult to get rid of without heavy sanding or patching. Here are a few ways to avoid the problem:

■ Don't submerge the roller in the paint to load it. Paint can seep inside the roller cover and leak out while you're rolling. Try to dip only the nap. Then spin it against the screen and dip again until the sleeve cover is loaded with paint.

■ Don't press too hard when you're smoothing out the paint.

■ Never start against an edge, like a corner or molding, with a full roller of paint. You'll leave a heavy buildup of paint that can't be spread out. Starting about 6 in. from the edge, unload the paint from the roller. Then work back toward the edge.

■ Unload excess paint from the open end of the roller before you roll back over the wall to smooth it out. Do this by tilting the roller and applying a little extra pressure to the open side of the roller while rolling it up and down in the area you've just painted.

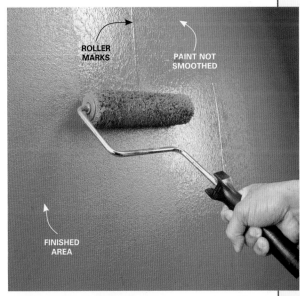

Smooth walls by rolling back over the wet paint without reloading the roller. Roll lightly without pressing.

5 Lay paint on wall areas above and below windows and doors with a long horizontal stroke. Then smooth it off with short vertical strokes so the texture will match the rest of the wall.

■ Pick out the lumps before they dry. It's inevitable that you'll end up with an occasional lump in your paint. Keep the roller cover away from the floor where it might pick up bits of debris that are later spread against the wall. Drying bits of paint from the edge of the bucket or bucket screen can also cause this problem. Cover the bucket with a damp cloth when you're not using it. If partially dried paint is sloughing off the screen, take it out and clean it. Keep a wet rag in your pocket and pick lumps off the wall as you go. Strain used paint through a mesh paint strainer to remove lumps. Five-gallon size strainers are available at paint stores.

■ Scrape excess paint from the roller before you wash it. Use your putty knife, or better yet, a special roller scraping tool with a semicircular cutout in the blade. Then rinse the roller cover until the water runs clear. A roller and paint brush spinning tool, available at hardware and paint stores, simplifies the cleaning task. Just slip the roller cover onto the spin- ner and repeatedly wet and spin out the roller until it's clean.

Spray paint revives old upholstery

Here's one way you can make an old chair look like new. Special spray paint formulated for fabric can hide stains, update the color of old solid-color upholstery and even obscure minor wear. It's available at most auto parts stores and some home centers and hard- ware stores. Most stores carry only two or three colors. To find more colors, do an online search for "fabric spray paint."

Fabric spray paint has one drawback: It can make fabric feel rough. This usually isn't a big problem with smooth fabrics, but fabric with a "nap," such as velour, may feel like sandpaper after painting. Test the back of a chair or the underside of a seat cushion before you paint the entire piece.

Painting **woodwork**

Having trouble getting your paint to look smooth? Welcome to the club. Painting woodwork so it has a flawless, glossy sheen is challenging. Here you'll learn some techniques and tricks that'll produce top-notch results.

For great painted woodwork, good surface preparation and good brushing technique are essential.

Many pros still rely solely on oil-based paints because they dry slowly and allow brush marks to flatten out. But you can achieve similar results with high-quality latex paint. Today's formulations cover and brush out well. You won't have the strong odor of oil that'll drive you out of the house for days. And latex also offers the advantage of fast drying and easy soap and water cleanup.

Latex paint is available in a range of sheens from flat to high gloss. Because you want your wood trim to wear well, use eggshell or semigloss. The downside to these shiny finishes is that every bump and scratch shows through.

1 Remove all loose or cracked paint with a stiff putty knife. Work in various directions to get underneath the loose paint.

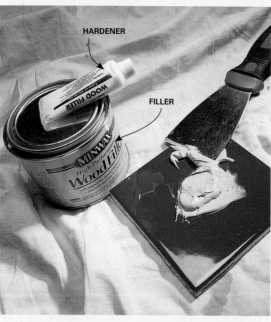

HARDENER

FILLER

2 Fill nicks and gouges with a two-part wood filler. Mix it thoroughly (following label directions) with a 2- or 3-in. flexible metal or plastic putty knife.

3 Pick up a dab of putty with the knife and apply it to the gouges. Hold the putty knife at an angle and press and smooth the filler into the scraped area. Leave the filler slightly higher than the surrounding surface.

Preparation, preparation

A coat of paint won't fill or hide cracks, chips and other surface defects, and it won't smooth an existing rough surface. You have to fill and smooth the woodwork first.

Wash the woodwork with a TSP solution (or TSP substitute), available at home centers and paint stores, to remove grease and grime. Mix according to the directions on the package and scrub with a sponge or rag. Be sure to rinse well with clear water to remove residues.

Next examine the surface for loose and cracked paint that'll need scraping. Many scraper types are available, but a 2-in. stiff putty knife works well for small areas (Photo 1). When you're done scraping, you'll be left with a rougher surface and a few more scratches and gouges than when you started. Don't worry—you'll fix these areas next.

For dents and chips deeper than about 1/8 in., use a two-part polyester resin. One example is Minwax wood filler. It sticks well, doesn't shrink and sands easily. It's also the best material for rebuilding chipped corners. Auto body fillers also work well.

Scoop out a golf ball–size amount onto a scrap piece of wood, cardboard or tile. Add the correct amount of hardener (follow the directions) and mix thoroughly but quickly (Photo 2). The resin only has a 5- to 10-minute working time.

For finer scratches and chips, use spackling compound. (Ready Patch by Zinsser is one brand used by many pros.) Don't use a lightweight compound; it doesn't stick to painted wood as well.

> **tip** Stiff putty knives work better for scraping; flexible putty knives work better for filling.

tip Brush marks in the old paint are particularly annoying and have to be sanded out, not filled.

"Spot-prime" the filler and any bare wood with a latex primer. This step is worth the effort because it helps you see imperfections. Check your work by holding a bright light (trouble light or flashlight) close to the woodwork (Photo 5). Every small bump and scratch will jump out. Circle the defects with a pencil or mark them with tape, then go back to the filler and sanding steps. Spot-prime and finish-sand these reworked areas.

Prep work requires patience, especially when you have to go back to an earlier step. What you decide is acceptable here is what you'll get in the finish coat. But keep in mind that the most critical eye will probably be yours.

Finish up the prep work by lightly sanding all areas that haven't been scraped and spot-primed. Use 180-grit paper or the fine sanding sponge. This will smooth out previous brush marks and scuff the surface to help the new coat of paint stick. Then wipe down the whole surface with a damp cloth to remove all the dust.

Caulk

Now that the filling, sanding and priming are done, caulk any long cracks and gaps (Photo 6). Use an acrylic latex caulk; it adheres well, remains flexible and cleans up with water. Cut the caulk tube at the very tip to leave a very small hole. You'll have better control of the caulk. Apply a bead of caulk that protrudes slightly above the crack or gap, then wipe it with a damp cloth wrapped around your finger. Wipe excess caulk off the cloth so you don't smear it on either side of the joint. You may have to wipe several times to produce a smooth, clean caulk line.

SANDING SPONGE

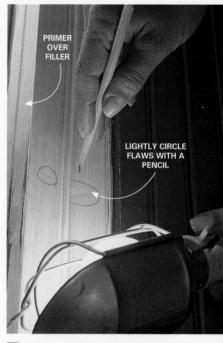

PRIMER OVER FILLER

LIGHTLY CIRCLE FLAWS WITH A PENCIL

4 Sand the filler flush to the painted surface with 100- or 120-grit sandpaper or a medium sanding sponge. Make sure to eliminate all ridges. Then finish-sand with 180-grit sandpaper or a fine sanding sponge. Spot-prime the filler and any bare wood.

5 Hold a trouble light close to the surface, and circle any imperfections with a pencil. Fill, sand and spot-prime these areas. Finally, lightly sand the entire surface with the 180-grit paper to ensure that the new paint will stick.

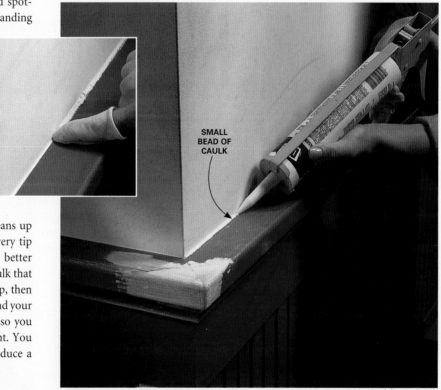

SMALL BEAD OF CAULK

6 Apply a small bead of paintable caulk to the crack between the wood and the wall. Smooth the caulk with a damp rag wrapped around your finger (inset). Wipe the edges to remove any ridges of caulk.

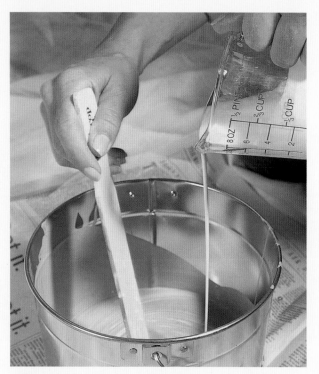

7 Pour a quart of paint into the pail and add a paint conditioner (such as Floetrol) for smoother results. Follow the label's instructions for the correct amount. Mix thoroughly.

8 Dip the brush bristles 1 to 2 in. into the paint to load the brush. Lightly tap the tip of the brush against the sides of the pail to shake off excess paint.

The paint and the brush

Don't undermine all the time and effort you've put into the prep work by using cheap brushes and paint. Buy the best. With proper cleaning, a quality brush will last for years. In most cases, you'll find the highest quality paint and tools (and good advice) at specialty paint stores.

Latex paint has one weakness: It dries quickly. The longer the paint remains wet, the better it flows and flattens, leaving a smooth surface. Use a paint conditioner or extender that slows down the drying process and helps the paint lie smooth. (Floetrol is one common choice; available at most paint stores.) Read the directions for the amount to add.

For best results from brushing, don't dip directly from the can. Pour a quart of the paint into a 4- or 5-qt. pail. This is your working paint that will move around with you. Add the measured amount of conditioner and mix well (Photo 7). From this pail you can dip and tap your brush without splattering. Good-quality paints are ready to use out of the can and don't need thinning with water. Be sure to have the paint store shake the can so it's well mixed, then stir the paint occasionally as you use it.

Brushing technique

The best sequence in brushing is to quickly coat an area with several brush loads of paint, and then blend and smooth it out by lightly running the unloaded brush tip over it (called "tipping"). See Photos 9 – 11, p. 139. Try to coat a whole board or section, but don't let the paint sit more than a minute before tipping.

The more paint the brush carries, the faster you'll coat the

Choosing a brush

As with paint, buy quality when you shop for brushes. For trim use a 2-1/2-in. straight brush and for detail work and cutting in, a 1-1/2-in. angle brush. For latex, buy a synthetic bristle brush with "exploded" tips. A good brush draws a decent "load" of paint into the bristles and applies it smoothly to the work surface.

STRAIGHT TIP

ANGLE TIP

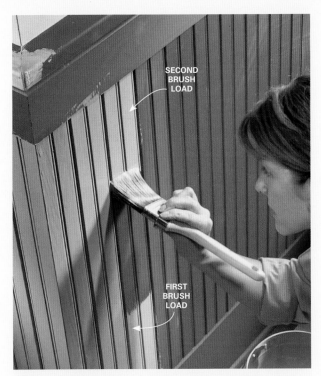

SECOND BRUSH LOAD

FIRST BRUSH LOAD

9 Start at the top of the board with the loaded brush and stroke down toward the middle. When the brush begins to drag, stop and reload.

10 "Tip" the wet paint by lightly setting the tip of the brush against the wet paint at the top of the board and lightly stroking down the whole length of the board. Hold the brush almost perpendicular to the surface for this stroke.

DIRECTION OF BRUSH STROKE

11 The fine brushstrokes left after tipping will flow together until the paint begins to skin over.

woodwork. But you want to avoid dripping. So after dipping, tap the tip of the brush against the pail, like the clapper of a bell (Photo 8). For a drier brush, try dragging one side over the edge of the pail.

Hold the brush at about a 45-degree angle, set the tip down where you want to start and pull it gently over the surface with a little downward pressure (Photo 9). Here's where the good brush pays off. The paint will flow smoothly onto the surface with little effort on your part. A common mistake is to force paint out of the brush after it becomes too dry. The goal is a uniform thickness but not so thick as to run or sag. With practice, you'll quickly find the ideal thickness. If the new color doesn't hide the old, it's better to apply a second coat than to apply the paint too thick. Continue the next brush load from where the last stroke left off, or work backward, say from an inside corner back into the wet paint.

When "tipping," avoid dabbing small areas as this leaves marks in the paint. Make long strokes. The brush will leave a slight track of parallel ridges, but they'll lie down before the paint begins to skin over (Photo 11).

Masking off and cutting in

Often the boards you're painting butt against a different paint color or a wall. There are a couple of ways to leave a sharp, crisp line.

Masking off with tape is one method. Lay painter's tape tight to the line where your new coat of paint will end (Photo 12). Push the tape tight against the surface with a putty knife to prevent the wet paint from bleeding (running) underneath the tape. Brush

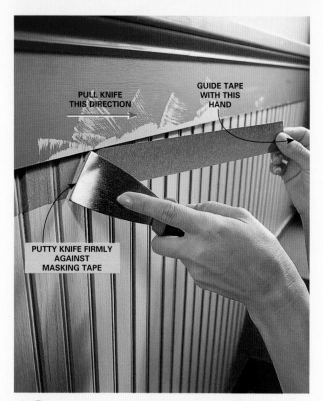

PULL KNIFE
THIS DIRECTION

GUIDE TAPE
WITH THIS
HAND

PUTTY KNIFE FIRMLY
AGAINST
MASKING TAPE

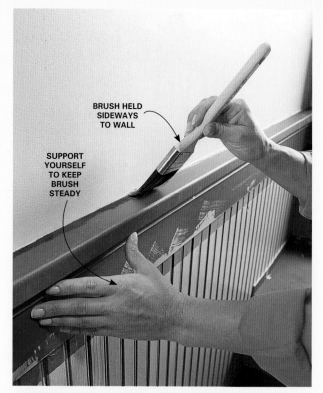

BRUSH HELD
SIDEWAYS
TO WALL

SUPPORT
YOURSELF
TO KEEP
BRUSH
STEADY

12 Apply painter's masking tape to protect finished surfaces before brushing on the second color. Carefully position the tape and push it tight against the surface with a putty knife. Be sure the paint underneath has thoroughly dried before taping.

13 Load the 1-1/2-in. brush with paint and drag one side over the edge of the pail. Holding the dry side of the brush toward the wall, carefully set the tip of the brush close to the wall line. Apply a little pressure and pull the brush along the line. Guide the paint up to the line by manipulating the pressure and position of the brush's tip as you pull it along.

the woodwork, letting the paint go partially onto the tape, then tip. Remove the tape when the paint is dry.

The pros usually skip the masking tape and just cut in with a brush; it's faster. With some practice and a steady hand, even an amateur can get very sharp lines. Learn with a smaller brush (1-1/2 in.) and go to a wider brush as you gain control. Dip the brush and scrape one side on the pail. Hold the dry side of the brush toward the wall and slowly draw the brush along (Photo 13). Support your arm to steady it, and keep the stroke moving. Use gentle downward pressure; you want the bristles to splay out slightly as you stroke. You'll find you can control the paint line by varying the pressure you apply to the brush.

When the brush is dry, reload and start where the previous stroke ended. Sometimes you'll have to go back over a section where the paint is shy of the wall. Complete cutting in and then coat the rest of the piece.

Finishing up

Whether one coat will suffice depends on the paint used and the color. If the first coat of paint looks streaky or transparent, a second coat is necessary. Let the previous coat of paint dry overnight, then lightly sand with 180- or 220-grit paper or a fine sanding sponge. Wash the dust off the surface with a damp cloth, let dry and brush on another coat.

Paint brush holder

Soak oil brushes in cleaning solvent without bending the bristles and ruining the brush! Clip a medium or large binder clip around the handle of a brush and spread the arms to span a cleaning container so the brush bristles don't touch the bottom.

BINDER
CLIP

9 tips for painting doors

LAG BOLTS

1 Lay the door flat to avoid drips and runs

For convenience, it's tempting to leave a door hanging on its hinges when you paint. But for a smooth finish, you have to lay it flat and remove the hinges, knobs and other hardware. With the door laid flat on saw-horses, you can spread paint more quickly and not worry about drips and paint sags. And you can still paint both sides in a day if you rest the door on lag screws.

Drill one 3/16-in. hole in the bottom of the door and two at the top, then drive 4-in. by 1/4-in. lag screws partway into the door. Spread the sawhorses apart just enough so that the door doesn't touch either side but rests entirely on the bolts. Paint the first side, then just rotate the door on the single bolt at the bottom of the door while holding the other two bolts.

Paint one side of the door, then grab the two lag bolts at the top and turn the door on the single bolt at the other end.

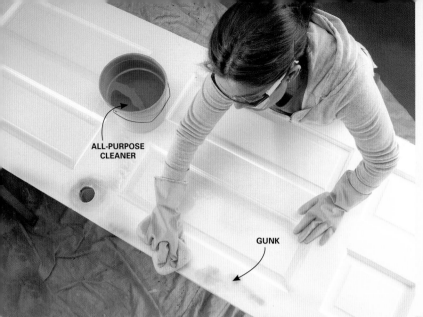

ALL-PURPOSE CLEANER

GUNK

2 Clean off grime before you prime

Washing your old finish is probably the most important step you can take to ensure good paint adhesion. Even the best paint won't stick well to oil and dirt, and there's lots of both on doors, especially near the knob, where dirty hands have pushed and pulled for years. Before filling holes or priming, scrub the entire door with heavy-duty household cleaner. Let the door dry completely, then fill any holes.

Scrub oil and dirt off the door so the primer can bond fully to the old paint.

3 Beware of paint buildup

Decades of paint buildup can make a door rub against the jamb or door stop molding. The fastest way to remove paint buildup is with a sharp stainless steel or carbide scraper.

After scraping, sand the door to smooth the scraped edges. Use power sanders sparingly—high-speed sanding can melt paint, making it even more difficult to smooth out.

Use sandpaper rather than a scraper on metal doors. Chemically strip fiberglass doors if they have flaking paint—you'll quickly ruin a fiberglass door (smooth or wood grain) if you scrape or sand it.

Scrape off thick paint buildup along the edges of doors to keep them from rubbing against the jamb or stop molding. Also scrape any flaking paint.

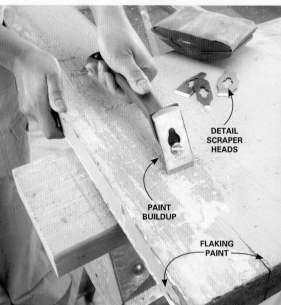

DETAIL SCRAPER HEADS

PAINT BUILDUP

FLAKING PAINT

4 Fill all holes, even small ones

You might assume that new paint will hide tiny dents and scratches, but it won't. In fact, the new coat of paint highlights minor flaws. Fill dents less than 1/8 in. deep with spackling compound. For deeper holes, use a two-part filler such as Minwax High Performance or an epoxy wood filler. It's more of a hassle to use and you usually end up throwing away a lot of partially hardened filler (mix small batches), but the patch will be hard enough to take a lot of abuse without falling out.

Force two-part filler into large or deep holes with a putty knife. Spread spackling compound over small, shallow holes and scratches.

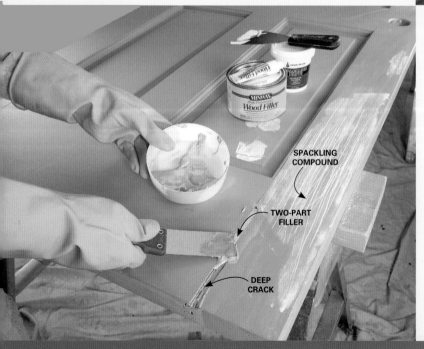

SPACKLING COMPOUND

TWO-PART FILLER

DEEP CRACK

5 Prime the entire door before painting

Unless the old paint is in perfect condition, you should prime before painting. Primer blocks stains, mutes dark colors and helps new paint stick better. It also seals porous fillers so the topcoat looks smooth and even. Avoid spot-priming—it will make the topcoat of paint look blotchy. If you're covering a color or painting on a new color (anything other than white), use a gray-tinted primer instead of a white primer.

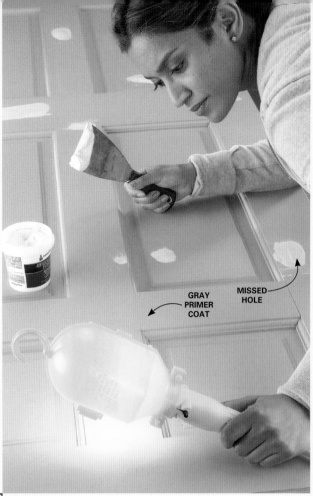

GRAY PRIMER COAT

MISSED HOLE

6 Search for flaws after priming

Minor flaws in your patching job are hard to see on an old painted surface, but they'll show up much better after a fresh coat of primer. After the primer dries, check the door again with a strong light. Cover any flaws with more spackling compound, then sand and reprime these areas with the same roller or brush, feathering the edges so the additional primer blends in.

Shine a light at a low angle across the door after priming to locate any missed scratches, dents or pinholes.

220-GRIT SANDING PAD

180-GRIT SANDPAPER

7 Sand between coats

No matter how careful you are, you can usually find ridges or bubbles or a few bits of dust and lint in a fresh coat of paint or primer. For the smoothest possible topcoat, hand-sand the entire door after the primer and between coats of paint. It may seem like a lot of work, but it shouldn't take more than five minutes when the door is flat on the sawhorses. Sand with nonclogging 180- or 220-grit sandpaper or sanding sponges (look for "nonclogging" or "stearated" on the label). Sand just enough to make the surface feel smooth. After sanding, vacuum and wipe down the door with a damp cloth to remove all the dust.

180-GRIT SANDPAPER

120-GRIT SANDPAPER

Lightly sand the entire door between coats with 180- to 220-grit paper. Use a sanding sponge for shaped areas.

8 Get a smoother finish with a mini roller

The best way to avoid brush marks is to avoid using brushes. High-density foam mini rollers spread paint smoothly and evenly, without brush marks and without the bumpy surface that standard-nap rollers leave. They also have rounded ends that almost eliminate lap marks and let you paint into corners without leaving scrapes or ridges.

Edge in around windows and panels with a brush first, then coat the rest of the door with the foam roller. Use the rollers for both primer and paint. They spread a thinner coat of paint than brushes or conventional rollers do, so you'll need at least two coats.

6" FOAM ROLLER

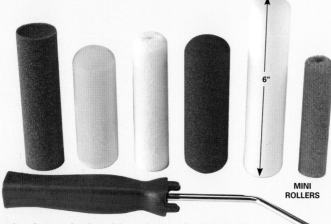

6"

MINI ROLLERS

4"

Apply primer and paint with a 4-in. or 6-in. high-density foam roller for a smoother finish.

9 Protect freshly painted doors from sticking

It's difficult to know how soon to put a door back up again after painting. And for home security, you'll want to get exterior doors back up as soon as possible. But even when latex paint is dry to the touch, it can still stick to the doorstop or weather stripping and then peel off when you open the door.

To be safe, wait at least two days before closing an interior door. This is especially true during humid conditions, when it takes longer for paint to cure properly. With an exterior door, either remove the weather stripping or cover it with painter's tape so the paint won't stick.

Cover weather stripping on an exterior door to prevent fresh paint from sticking to the weather stripping.

PAINTER'S TAPE

DRY BUT NOT CURED